THE GOOD COMPANY

Compassionate Companies That Are
Changing the World

Revised Edition

Robert H. Girling Ph.D.

If you earnestly desire your own welfare,

First seek that of others.

He that seeks only his own benefit

Will not succeed in his purpose.

Sakya Pandita

This book is dedicated to the memory of

my mother who taught me to look for the positive in every situation, my father who nurtured my early interest in business and to my children and grandchildren and all who are working to make the world a better place.

That only which we have within, can we see without. If we meet no gods, it is because we harbor none.

Emerson

WHAT OTHERS HAVE TO SAY ABOUT *"THE GOOD COMPANY"*

Robert Girling offers a refreshing perspective on reconfiguring business practices in "The Good Company." By offering numerous case studies of revolutionary best practices, he creates a road map towards transforming myopic short-term profit-driven institutions into those which accept their broader social responsibilities where moral and ethical behavior become fundamental drivers of competitive advantage. This book profiles many who are leading this transformation while offering hope for the future of our planet and our communities. It is a must-read for anyone concerned about building a sustainable future.

David Wylie, Executive in Residence Babson College

The Good Company, traces a new corporate business model based on a very old philosophical principle and ethic—"ahimsa" or do no harm. A growing number of corporations have discovered that by doing good and not harm they do well. They are learning to exercise conscious or consequence sensitive decision making which supports what he states are the "The Triple Bottom Line" of people, planet, and profit. "The Good Company" is more than a lesson in corporate social responsibility.

Tom DiGrazia, J.D., Adjunct Professor, Mediation and Conflict, Hawaii Pacific University

This book explores why and how some companies contribute to the common good. It doesn't shy away from exploring legislative and other barriers for companies. There are lots of examples to illustrate what real companies are doing to improve their financial bottom line while contributing to the well-being of the planet, their communities and their employees. Investors and consumers can use those examples to make decisions and current and future business owners will find the examples inspiring.

Merith Weisman, Center for Community Engagement, Sonoma State University

TABLE OF CONTENTS

THE GOOD COMPANY

COMPANY

Compassionate Companies That Are Changing the World

PREFACE

For much of my adult life I have been researching good organizations. By "good organizations," I mean companies, non-profits, and government agencies that seek to change a multitude of irrational patterns in business and in the economy. This quest has taken me around the world in a variety of professional and travel experiences, and has led me to work as a development economist, teacher, and social entrepreneur—work that culminates now with the birth of this book.

I was born in the island of Jamaica where my family had resided for over 200 years. Early in my life my parents decided to move to California in search of educational opportunities and as a result, I attended the University of California in Berkeley and then traveled to England to the University of Essex in England, where I studied economic development. Upon completing my degree in England in 1968, I returned to my native Jamaica where I had the opportunity to learn firsthand about the practice of economic development.

And learn I did!

Jamaica, at the time, having just been granted independence from Great Britain, was just emerging from 250 years of colonialism. I immediately became involved in the attempt to transform the economy as part by joining the small staff of the newly created National Planning Agency, then attached to the office of the Minister of Finance. My work in creating an economic strategy for Jamaica's development under the direction of Gladstone Bonnick provided me vast opportunities to learn about Jamaica's reality.

As director for regional planning, I traveled from one end of the small island to the other trying to understand how the economy operated. I met with colleagues from all branches of the Jamaican government, representatives of the commercial sector, and a group of leading thinkers like George Beckford, Alistair MacIntyre, and Norman Girvan at the University of the West Indies. At the NPA we studied the impact of business on the Jamaican economy from tourism to the growing bauxite industry. And, in the course of my work, I learned about the harsh realities of slum dwellers like Clive Johnson, a tall, gaunt 35-year-old who I met one day strolling down the street on my lunch break. Like thousands of others like him, he had never been able to hold gainful employment; Clive lived a life on the edge, inhabiting a 6-by-8 foot shack built of corrugated iron sheets in the midst of Kingston's shantytown. Every day, his situation reminded me of the plight of the unemployed.

I wanted to learn more about why so many like Clive were left behind. I began to wonder what it would take to create industries and companies that could provide meaningful opportunities to the growing army of marginalized people in the Third World. As it turned out, I had an opportunity to do just that when the Ford Foundation provided me with a scholarship to pursue doctoral studies at Stanford University's International Development Education Center, where I wrote my thesis on Jamaica's food processing industry. I sought to understand how it was that a land as rich and fertile as Jamaica failed to feed its people or provide them with work.

While studying at Stanford, I also had the opportunity to work with a number of outstanding faculty members including Martin Carnoy, St.Clair Drake, Clark Reynolds, Frank Bonilla, Hans Weiler as well as visiting professor Fernando Henrique Cardoso, who had written about dependent development as a paradigm for understanding the dominant-dependent relationship between industrialized and developing countries and later went on to be elected President of Brazil[1]. This work, in turn, led me to examine the operations of multinational

---

[1] Along with Brazil's former President Fernando Henrique Cardoso, Professor Frank Bonilla and a group of Brazilian students including Benecio Schmidt and Evelina Dagnino, in 1972 I co-edited a book "Structures of Dependency," which explored Cardoso's theory. Cardoso was elected President of Brazil in 1994.

companies operating in Jamaica. My conclusion was that these companies exhibited little regard for their 'host' country and the people who lived there, and displayed little of what we today call "corporate social responsibility."

On my return to Jamaica in 1974, I was asked to prepare plans for a Special Employment Program to address the growing wave of unemployment, which stood at the alarming rate of 18 percent. I drew together a task force of experts from different parts of the Jamaican government and we set to work identifying a public employment program modeled in part on US President Franklin Roosevelt's depression era Works Project Administration [WPA], and setting economic criteria for good projects that would add jobs or conserve natural resources. [2]

Meanwhile, as the former economic domination of the British was passing to the United States, a host of international experts began to arrive monthly. The World Bank and the Inter-American Development Bank mediated this changeover process. Project loans quickly added to Jamaica's growing mountain of debt as the management of Jamaica's economy shifted from Kingston to Washington DC[3]. My frustration at this point mounted daily.

Fortuitously, at this time, a group of Brazilian colleagues from Stanford including Glaura Miranda, Isaura Belloni and Benicio Schmidt who were now at the Federal University of Minas Gerais Brazil invited my wife and I to join them in starting a new Master's program. Although a challenge, especially in view of my minimal Portuguese, I grabbed hold of this opportunity to expand my horizons. At the end of my year in Brazil, I was offered a job in the School of Business and Economics at Sonoma State University.

---

[2] A detailed summary of this program appears in "The Planning, and Management of Jamaica's Special Employment Program: Lessons and Limitations," Social and Economic Studies, Vol. 29, No. 2, June 1980. The broader framework is discussed in my article, "Technology and Development in Jamaica: A Case Study," Social and Economic Studies, June 1977.

[3] I have dealt with this in some detail in my book, "Multinational Institutions and the Third World: Management of Debt and Trade Conflicts in the International Economic Order," published by Praeger Publishers, New York, 1985. However, a more recent and comprehensive picture of the process by which the economies of developing countries were ensnared and dominated by a perverse economic system is contained in John Perkin's excellent book, "Confessions of An Economic Hit Man," Penguin, 2005.

While teaching at Sonoma State University, I expanded my search for examples of all types of good companies, organizing a conference on Democratic Management that focused on worker cooperatives. I had a number of opportunities to observe effective and ineffective management while consulting with the United Nations, The World Bank and the International Center for Research on Women [ICRW]. Then later while teaching at the Federal University of Bahia along with a group of colleagues including Sherry Keith, Katia Freitas and Bob Verhine, we spent over a decade developing LIDERE, a program for improving the quality of school management in Northeast Brazil with funding from the Ford Foundation. LIDERE was a program designed to provide schools in Northeast Brazil with the management skills they needed to deal with a particularly difficult social reality ranging from poor buildings and facilities to lack of trained teachers. The program worked to strengthen educational leadership in schools in Northeast Brazil by providing training in team building, budgeting, school planning, educational evaluation, curriculum and communication while also assisting municipalities in democratizing the management of schools. I learned from this experience that if you set a worthy and important goal, good people will flock to assist you. I learned the value of the demonstration effect; by demonstrating that there was another way, that schools could improve with the participation of teachers, the project caught the attention of local and state government. The program grew to touch the lives of an estimated 30,000 students at 80 schools; the Ford Foundation also recognized the program as one of its 10 outstanding social projects worldwide. This experience led me in search of examples of social enterprises around the world[4].

In 2002, a colleague and I began studying social enterprises, companies and non-profits that were part of a growing trend in social investment and innovation[5]. As we searched, we discovered more and more examples of organizations that

---

[4] Paul Hawken in his book Blessed Unrest, estimates that there are over 1 million such organizations working to do good.

[5] As a result of this work I published several papers: "Global Innovators" in *SMEs and Open Innovation: Global Cases and Initiatives;* Haikikur Rahman ed. 2011;"Teaching Green Business: How to Bring Sustainability into a Capstone Business Class" in *Management Education for Global Sustainability (PB) (Research in Management Education and Development)* ; Charles Wankel and James A F Stoner eds.; "Global Innovators: How Some Companies are Working to Improve Social Conditions Around the World" Journal of Applied Business and Economics, 2009 and L.Thach, R. Girling, & D. Svarcev, D. "Adoption of Sustainable Business Practices in Small to Medium-Sized Organizations." Regional Business Review, Volume 27.2008

exhibited a caring orientation including for-profit, non-profit, and hybrid organizations that were invested in building healthy communities, promoting social justice and protecting the environment. Through my research I met a number of business leaders in who were involved in changing the face of business. It seemed that everywhere we looked we found examples of companies and organizations truly devoted to meeting human needs.

Today, you hold in your hand, or view on your screen, the result of that search, and the work and experiences that came before it. I hope that these stories of good companies inspire you to dream of even bigger and bolder ideas that will shape the companies of tomorrow.

INTRODUCTION

Fresh out of college, Jeff Mendelsohn was determined to make a difference with his work. Rather than chasing a fortune, he chose to start a business that would make the world a better place. It was the early 1990s and the world was again in recession. Mendelsohn was shocked by the reality facing the poor countries of Central America—and particularly the rampant deforestation of the rainforests. Yet he was also inspired to search for a real solution.

Mendelsohn's search led him to set his sights on the paper industry, known for its voracious destruction of forests and its pollution of streams and rivers. After graduation, armed with his values and his vision, he got a job with a start-up: New York Recycled Paper. Mendelsohn's goal was not just to transform the company but to shift the entire paper industry. Six months later, he purchased the fledgling business for $2,000. "I decided that the best thing was to form a mission-based company that would be a model for other companies." After moving the company to San Francisco in 1998, he renamed it New Leaf Paper. From the outset the company was values-driven with the mission of leading a shift toward sustainability in the paper industry.

The company aimed to embed its social and environmental values into every product line and every business relationship. New Leaf Paper was first to market 100% post-consumer recycled coated papers, and book publishing papers. By 2001 the first book was published with 100 percent recycled paper. In 2003 Harry Potter and the Order of the Phoenix came out on New Leaf recycled paper and in 2005 three leading paper companies followed New Leaf's lead. Its product innovation and market success caused major paper manufacturers to take notice and change their paper, indirectly widening New Leaf Paper's environmental impact.

Now more than ever the world needs businesses like New Leaf Paper. People are tired of mega-banks and corporations that are driven solely by profit and not a desire to produce needed products at a fair price. The public's trust in business has reached a new low with only 10% of Americans saying they trust large companies and 77% asserting that they would refuse to buy products or services from a company they distrust.[6]

Our values and expectations are changing. We need companies that reflect the change in our values and expectations toward corporate behavior and the environment. The good news is that there are a growing number of companies like Mendelsohn's out there—*good companies*— working to repair the damage and heal the world. Some companies do this by prioritizing social justice, treating their employees fairly and with respect and restoring Planet Earth. These companies—good companies—act based on a honor and respect for fellow beings while also keeping an eye on the financial bottom line. They are motivated by trust and cooperation rather than fear and cut-throat competition. Good companies see the unlimited possibilities of the world. In relationships with stakeholders, they seek to replace unequal power and unequal exchange with the concept of partnership. They take risks to do what is right.

Why do good companies care—and how do they care—for their communities, employees, and planet? What actions have they taken and what have they accomplished? And what lessons can we learn from them? In the following chapters, we will explore these questions and more, journeying through a sampling of the many social enterprises, for-profit companies and non-profits that are putting values and ethics back into business. Who are these people and why are these *good companies*? What

---

[6] Shoshana Zuboff."The Old Solutions Have Become the New Problems;" Bloomberg Businessweek. July 2, 2009

distinguishes them from the others? I have set out to tell you the stories of some of the most innovative companies that are healing their communities and the planet.

In chapter one, I explain why we need a new 21st Century approach to business and I identify some organizations that are leading the movement toward change. In chapter two, I define the "good company" and explain how and why they are more successful than traditional organizations.

In chapters three through nineteen, I tell the stories of companies that excel in taking care of their employees, their communities and the planet. By incorporating these transformative values into their DNA, companies like Vestergaard-Frandsen and TOMS Shoes are helping to eliminate some of the world's most insidious diseases while Triodos Bank points the way to a progressive financial system that serves and supports communities. Interface Carpets is one such company that has instigated a culture shift by reducing waste, recycling, and reusing scarce natural resources. Companies like INDIGENOUS and Kiva illustrate how innovative business practices can produce change that lifts millions out of poverty.

The concluding chapters 20 and 21 help you ponder—and begin to answer—the two questions: "Where do I start to build a good company?" and "What is being done to create more good companies?"

New Leaf Paper has generated environmental benefits and promoted the company's greater mission by pioneering markets and shifting the behavior of its competitors. Moreover, the company has saved over 2 million trees and a half billion gallons of water while making a profit every year since it was founded.

The companies whose stories appear in this book are but a few of the many that are changing our world. They represent the heart and soul of a new breed of business that incorporate core values into their identities and cultures, they seek to honor employees, to respect the environment, to give back to their communities, to provide value to their customers, and to be consistently profitable.

I've created each chapter to be self-contained, providing you with insights as well as inspiration. You can read any one of these stories and come away with a certainty that there is hope for the future.

CHAPTER ONE

TWENTY-FIRST CENTURY COMPANIES

The 21ˢᵗ century began with a wave of corporate scandals and financial meltdowns. It started in 2001 with the collapse of Enron, previously rated by Fortune Magazine as America's most innovative company for six years in a row. This was followed by Arthur Andersen in 2002, found guilty of criminal charges related to its auditing of Enron. Then came scandals in insurance and mutual funds and then in 2008 the collapse of major banks around the world. Trillions of dollars of equity turned to smoke.

In 2010 oil giant BP chose to put profits before people by installing a substandard safety valve in order to save $500 million. This for a company whose annual profit in 2009 was already $14 billion.[7] The resulting damage to the environment and the lives of employees has been estimated as upwards of $20 billion.[8]

---

[7] BP Delivers on Promises in "Very Good" 2009 as 4Q Profits Jump 70 percent
http://www.bp.com/extendedgenericarticle.do?categoryId=2012968&contentId=7059471
[8] BP Oil Spill Cost Hits $40 Billion, Company Returns To Profit Brian Skoloff and Jane Wardell .
http://www.huffingtonpost.com/2010/11/02/bp-oil-spill-costs-hit-40_n_777521.html

The wave of unethical behavior among financial institutions and banks like Barclays and Bank of America, accounting firms like Arthur Anderson, regulatory agencies like the Securities Exchange Commission and even rating agencies like Moody's that we depend on to monitor the behavior of banks and corporations has demonstrated that the dysfunction in our economic system runs deep.[9]

The Occupy Wall Street movement which started in 2011 called attention to a production system that is seen as deeply unjust, irrational and out of control. Driven by a drive to increase profits and a lack of respect for the environment, global banks and corporations have trashed the planet. In a manner reminiscent of the Great Depression, the billionaires and mega-banks have amassed wealth but lost interest in investments that provide meaningful employment, restore the planet and build a strong economy. The Occupy movement stands for policies that would create jobs while addressing inequities and corporate dominance and the destruction of the environment.

Author and businessman Paul Hawken has dedicated his life to changing the relationship between business and the environment. His work includes starting and running ecological businesses, as well as writing and teaching about the impact of commerce on the environment.

In Hawken's influential book *The Ecology of Commerce* he cautions that, "Quite simply, our business practices are destroying life on earth. Given current corporate practices, not one wildlife reserve, wilderness, or indigenous culture will survive the global market economy." Even more apocalyptically, as he warns later in the same book, "We know that every natural system on the planet is disintegrating. The land, water, air, and the sea have been functionally transformed from life-supporting systems into repositories for waste. There is no polite way to say that business is destroying the world."[10]

---

[9] Les Leopold. The Looting of America: How Wall Street's Game of Fantasy Finance Destroyed our Jobs, Pensions, and Prosperity. Chelsea Green. 2009

[10] Paul Hawken, The Ecology of Commerce: A Declaration of Sustainability (New York: HarperBusiness, 1993)Hawken also heads the Natural Capital Institute (NCI), a research oriented NGO located in Sausalito, California. NCI's projects include the documentary film "Blessed Unrest" based upon Hawken's book, and the first open source database of the hundreds of thousands of organizations

Business and society are at a crossroads. With each passing day it becomes evident to thought leaders around the world that business—as it has been practiced in the United States and much of the world—is on the wrong path. Dominated by narrow self-interest, greed, arrogance, and insensitivity to the greater good, the old style of business has brought us to the brink; the financial collapse of 2008 and the following recession has come at a tremendous human cost. As Peter Blom, Chairman of the Executive Board of Triodos Bank put it, "We have to transform our thinking about the economy [in a way] that combines ecological-economic-social dimensions...." [11]

Clearly the world cries out for repair. Consider that nearly half the world lives in a state of poverty while just one fifth consume over 80 percent of the worlds resources.[see Sidebar]

It is clear that business needs new values. Growing inequalities have undermined our communities.

About 20% of the population in the developed nations consume 86% of the world's goods.

The poorest 40% of the world's population accounts for 5% of the global income. The richest 20% accounts for 75% of world income.

Nearly half the world – over three billion people – live on less than $2.50 a day.

About 1.1 billion people in developing countries have inadequate access to water, and 2.6 billion lack basic sanitation.

About 1.6 billion people – a quarter of humanity – live without electricity.

Of the 1.9 billion children from the developing world: 640 million are without adequate shelter, 400 million do not have access to safe water, 270 million do not have access to health services.

There is a groundswell of dissatisfaction with the corporation by customers, employees, shareholders and the community. The idea of the corporation that cares only about the bottom line and profit maximization is as outdated as the typewriter.

---

around the world dedicated to environmental restoration and social justice, available at www.wiserearth.org. NCI recently conducted a large research project on the subject of socially responsible investing (SRI) and created the first public database of SRI funds in North America, displaying complete company portfolios and screening categories. The research report describes the current state of SRI, and presents several recommendations to improve the industry.

[11] Address to the Presencing Institute. "MIT Green Hub and Peter Blom" April 27,2009. www.presencing.com

Still we remain trapped in an outmoded system which evolved from the halcyon 1920s when success was viewed solely in terms of short-term financial performance. What is missing is the consideration of important customer and societal needs—the protection of the natural environment, the economic needs of communities, and the need for safe working conditions for employees. Even Harvard Business School strategists are worried. In the Harvard Business Review, Michael Porter and Mark Kramer write "A narrow conception of capitalism has prevented business from harnessing its full potential to meet society's broader challenges."[12]

Consumers today want to know that the companies we work for and support are ethical and responsible. It's not enough to know how other business leaders rank companies. We need to know how business decisions affect our communities and the common good. We want to know how the businesses we patronize impact the environment, and how they influence poverty and social welfare.

David Batstone, a founding editor of Business 2.0, notes, "Corporate workers from the mailroom to the highest executive office express dissatisfaction with their work. They feel crushed by widespread greed, selfishness, and quest for profit at any cost.... [Employees] want to be part of something that matters and contribute to the greater good."[13] Even worse, when employees

> According to UNICEF, 26,500-30,000 children die each day due to poverty – that's 18 children dying every minute, a child every three seconds.
>
> Over 11 million children die each year from preventable causes like malaria, diarrhea and pneumonia.
>
> Income inequality, even in the rich OECD countries— which sparked the Occupy Wall Street movement in the U.S. — is widening. The richest 10 percent of the population earn nine times the average income of the poorest decile.
>
> **Sources:**
> http://www.dosomething.org/tip sandtools/11-facts-about-global-poverty;
> http://www.bloomberg.com/new s/2011-12-05/rich-poor-divide-is-widening-oecd-says.html

---

[12] Michael Porter and Mark Kramer. "Creating shared value." Harvard Business Review. Jan-Feb. 2011 p. 64.

[13] David Batstone. Preserving Integrity, Profitability, and Soul" in Joan Gallos, Business Leadership. Jossey Bass 2008

feel ashamed of their organizations, few will work to promote the company's strategy.[14]

Woody Tasch, chairman of Investors' Circle, a network of venture capitalists, angel investors and foundations, tells us that to fix our economy "we need a market that rewards companies that do not build value on broken relationships and whose value-creation process is built around the preservation and restoration of relationships: relationships between individuals, relationships between producers and consumers and communities, relationships between cultures, relationships between species. We need a market that puts the *share* back into shareholder, recognizing that it is no longer advisable, no longer prudent, or, even, no longer moral for the current generation of the beneficiaries of economic growth to take all or most of their profits off the table for their own use...."[15]

Employees want to work for ventures they believe are contributing to a better world. The idea of simply earning a living is not enough. They also want the opportunity to support and work for companies that actively do _good_. And they will not be satisfied with less than the opportunity to work within noble companies.

> **UNITED NATIONS GLOBAL COMPACT**
>
> **Principle 1**: Businesses should support and respect the protection of internationally proclaimed human rights;
>
> **Principle 2**: make sure that they are not complicit in human rights abuses.
>
> **Principle 3**: Businesses should uphold the freedom of association and the effective recognition of the right to collective bargaining;
>
> **Principle 4**: the elimination of all forms of forced and compulsory labor;
>
> **Principle 5**: the effective abolition of child labor; and
>
> **Principle 6**: the elimination of discrimination in respect of employment and occupation.
>
> **Principle 7**: Businesses should support a precautionary approach to environmental challenges;
>
> **Principle 8**: undertake initiatives to promote greater environmental responsibility; and
>
> **Principle 9**: encourage the development and diffusion of environmentally friendly technologies.
>
> **Principle 10**: Businesses should work

---

[14] Walker Loyalty Report 2007
[15] Woody Tasch. Inquiries into the Nature of Slow Money. Chelsea Green Press 2008. P. 136-7

I have observed that when companies relegate the profit motive to its proper role—as one among several factors that guide business decisions—then employees will give their best. Employees today expect more from the workplace; they expect fairness, compassion, and respect for nature.

Many companies grapple with these issues, and some tackle them with integrity. More than 300 companies worldwide have signed on to the UN Global Compact, a voluntary policy initiative for businesses committed to aligning their operations and strategies with ten universally accepted principles in the areas of human rights, labor, environment, and anti-corruption. (see sidebar)

Beyond the Fortune 500, a quiet revolution is occurring. Largely unreported, a growing number of small companies, and a few larger firms, non-profits, and social ventures are reaching out to heal our society and planet. Their efforts address the pressing challenges society faces: poverty, inequality, illiteracy, violence, healthcare, climate change. Even a few global companies such as Google are also taking bold steps to change how companies work, funneling a portion of revenues into alleviating poverty and advancing solar energy.

We need companies that believe that the true purpose of business is to add value to the community. As Ben Cohen, co-founder of Ben and Jerry's, and Mal Warwick remind us in their book *Values-driven Business*, "The true purpose of business is to add value—not just by transforming raw materials into goods or providing useful services but also by adding value to the lives of employees, adding value to the life of the community, and adding value for the sake of future generations by treading as lightly as possible on the planet."[16]

Business today faces three main challenges:

A human challenge -- To make sure that the way we do business meets the human needs of employees and communities.

An environmental challenge -- To create environmentally sustainable technologies, productions systems, and companies.

A global challenge – To develop a globally just economy that serves the common good around the world.

---

[16] Ben Cohen and Mal Warwick. Values –driven Business. Berrett-Koehler publishers. 2006 p.xvii.

We need companies that exist for the purpose of meeting these challenges, restoring our communities, repairing our ecosystems, and providing meaningful work.

Beneficial Companies

One group of businesses comprised of the leaders of over 400 companies are building a network dedicated to using the power of business to meet these challenges. They first assembled in San Francisco in March 2008 to declare the birth of B-net, where Jay Coen Gilbert, B-lab founder and former CEO of AND 1, $250M basketball footwear and apparel company launched the meeting with a challenge.

"We are setting out tonight to transform the economic landscape. Today people around the world are declaring the intention that they want business to benefit people and benefit the environment. …We are forming a network of beneficial corporations which will work to serve society and to maximize not just the interests of a small band of investors and executives, but will form a collective voice to maximize the interests of society. Our companies will work to distribute their wealth equitably among all who contribute to its creation and will respect the universal human rights."

Adam Lowry, CEO of Method, a home products manufacturer that produces child-safe cleaning products added "our companies will operate on a moral and ethical basis; that's our competitive advantage." Companies in the network must meet rigorous standards of social and environmental performance and commit to expand corporate accountability to include the consideration of employee, community and environmental interests in their decision making.

Yet B-net is not the only organization out to change the face of business. Corporation 20/20, an international initiative whose goal is to develop and disseminate a vision for corporations in which social purpose moves from the periphery to the heart of the organization, is another. Marjorie Kelly, editor of Business Ethics magazine and one of the founders of the Corporation 20/20 group put it this way:

"We need to move beyond the regulatory approach to containing the bad things that companies do to redesign the corporation for the 21st century. Our present model pays too much attention to the consequences and not enough to causes and incentives. We need to look at the roots of our system that is undermining our economy and poisoning our atmosphere. We need a new genus of business which is designed to promote a social mission as well as an economic one."[17]

Business executives are forced to focus on quarterly returns and cost cutting at the expense of product quality and employee welfare in order to boost revenues. Companies short-term gains in share price come at the cost of layoffs for employees. Meanwhile firms fail to invest in environmental sustainability measures that can produce long-term corporate and community returns.

Companies that remain trapped in an outdated approach to value creation undermine our economy and our communities. According to Porter and Kramer, such companies "continue to view value creation narrowly, optimizing short-term financial performance in a bubble while missing the most important customer needs and ignoring the broader influences that determine their longer-term success. How else could companies overlook the well-being of their customers, the depletion of natural resources vital to their businesses, the viability of key suppliers, or the economic distress of the communities in which they produce and sell?"[18]

Yet despite the fact that much work still needs to be done, we may take heart in the many valuable and unique lessons of companies that are changing the world. Their stories need to be told.

Over the past decades, in the course of teaching, advising and consulting, I have become aware of this emerging model of *good* business. I've encountered hundreds of companies such as Traditional Medicinals, The Semco Group, Clif Bar, Eileen Fisher, Better World Telcom, and Seventh Generation that are dedicated to a positive future based on principles of cooperation, economic justice, and sustainability to achieve true global security.

---

[17] BALLE Conference University of California; June 2007.

[18] Michael Porter and Mark Kramer. "Creating shared value." Harvard Business Review. Jan-Feb. 2011 p. 64.

Oded Gradjev, President of Brazil's Ethics Institute, says good companies are those that do the right thing and provide an environment in which employees do the right thing. "It's a process which never ends."

Meeting the human, economic, social and environmental challenges which face us will require sustained cooperation and strategic alliances between governments, foundations, international agencies, non-profits, companies and social enterprises. There is evidence of a growing movement to construct a new pattern of cooperation and new opportunities in the world of business and among non-profits.

The following chapters tell the stories of the new breed of companies around the world that are changing the way we do business and the way in which some businesses do good. This is the story of good companies.

CHAPTER 2

WHAT IS A GOOD COMPANY?

The problem is that in a narrowly defined business practice, the tendency is to measure results solely in financial terms and not in how the business is meeting people's needs. It is this kind of one-sided thinking that allows businesses to pollute the environment and destroy natural resources and that can cause discrimination and violence, as well as a sense of defeat in people's hearts, homes, and throughout the world.

Marc Lesser, ZBA:The Zen of Business Administration.

Clif Bar & Company, an American business that today is one of the world's best known brands, started out as a small bakery named Kali's Sweets & Savories selling calzones. In 1990, owner Gary Erickson went on a day-long, 175 mile bike ride. Partway through the ride, despite his gnawing hunger, he could not take another bite of the chalky energy bar. Erickson decided he could do better. Two years later, after much experimentation in his mother's kitchen, Erickson settled on a recipe for the Clif Bar, named after his father. In September 1991, Erickson introduced the Clif Bar in three flavors at a bicycle show. In its first year, fueled primarily by strong sales in bike shops and the growth of the health foods movement, sales of Clif Bar exceeded $700,000. Sales doubled each year, and by 1997, revenue surpassed $20 million.

Today Clif Bar is among the leading makers of organic energy and nutrition foods. Erickson and his wife, Kit built their company using a business model that integrates its socially responsible values into every area of the business. They've achieved a remarkable 10-year compounded annual growth rate of 23 percent. The company gained national acclaim for its commitment to the environment and its support for important causes such as the fight against breast cancer. It is also renowned for its treatment of employees. [19]

Outside magazine named the company to its list of Best Places to Work in 2008, 2009, and 2010. Health magazine named Clif Bar & Company the "Healthiest Company for Women to Work For." And Fortune Small Business added Erickson to its list of *Best Bosses in America.*[20]

Why all the acclaim? The company transmits its values. Since 2001, Clif Bar has doggedly pursued its goal to conduct every aspect of its business sustainably. "I have a responsibility to the people of Clif Bar," said Erickson. "We want to sustain a business where people can live, not just make a living. We believe that if we provide meaningful work as well as something beyond work, people will do their jobs well and lead healthier, more balanced lives." Clif Bar's focus on health, well-being, and sustainability sets it apart from the average company. Erickson willingly turned down the opportunity to make $60 million by selling Clif Bar so he could fulfill his vision of a sustainable business.

Seeking to reduce its ecological footprint, Clif Bar set a goal to build an ecological company, one that would work with nature and conserve the planet's resources. The company set out to reduce its packaging material, offset carbon dioxide emissions with wind energy and partner with a host of environmental organizations such as the Organic Farming Research Foundation. In 2004, Clif Bar received the EPA's Green Power Partner of the Year Award, EPA's highest honor for buyers of "green power," or electricity created by renewable resources. Clif Bar also won the StopWaste Efficiency Award from the Alameda Waste Management Authority, an honor that rewards corporate efforts to recycle, compost, and prevent waste. In April

---

[19] http://findarticles.com/p/articles/mi_m1016/is_4_112/ai_n27149281/ and Good Business Network. Stirring It Up & Raising the Bar: A Conversation with Clif Bar & Company and Stonyfield Farm www.goodbusinessnetwork.com
[20] www.clifbar.com

2009, Clif Bar joined BICEP, a coalition of 18 companies with the goal of passing progressive climate and energy legislation.

"At Clif Bar we have created a business model that looks well beyond the bottom line," said Erickson. "We are a vision-centric company and we work hard to not only sustain our brand and business, but our people, our community, and our planet."[21]

Good Companies Prioritize People, Communities, Planet And Profits

In this book I use the term good company to convey the concept of a business that looks beyond the private profit that benefits shareholders and investors to include the welfare of employees who produce the products and services (as well as those of its suppliers), the community that hosts the company, and the environment that supplies the natural resources.

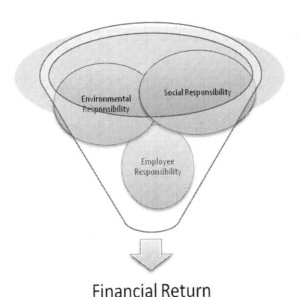

Financial Return

Figure 2.1 Good Companies Benefit From Responsibility

---

21 http://findarticles.com/p/articles/mi_m1016/is_4_112/ai_n27149281/ and Good Business Network

Figure 2.1 illustrates how good companies benefit from responsible behavior. Beginning with economic/employee responsibility, i.e. fair treatment of employees by providing fair wages and a safe workplace, companies lay a foundation for success. Beyond that, to be socially responsible, the company will undertake and support beneficial activities and practices in the community. It will also engage in environmental responsibility with a focus on reducing environmental harm through recycling, waste reduction, avoiding harmful production and use of toxic chemicals, and reducing energy consumption. Furthermore, in order to sustain itself, a company must generate a financial return or income in excess of its expenditures.

According to conventional 20th century business practices, an organization's long-term viability has been measured solely on profitability, the bottom line. Many companies still assess themselves annually according to that out-dated model. However, today we know different. We know that true long-term success depends on a broader, more inclusive set of criteria. This has led to the notion of the triple or quadruple bottom-line.[22]

Multiple bottom line reporting views the company to be responsible and accountable to all stakeholders, not just the investors or shareholders. The stakeholders of an organization include anyone who is affected by the business activities of a company including shareholders, customers, employees, the community and suppliers.[23]

To summarize, good companies focus on serving their customers by caring for their employees and the community. In order to do this, they treat employees fairly while making contributions to the community, care for the planet, and are profitable going-concerns.

However, while the methodology for measuring financial aspects such as earnings, revenues and costs, are long established and predominate the language of business, we lack established methods to quantify social and environmental aspects. For example, how should we measure the

---

[22] see D. Brown, J.Dillard and R.S. Marshall. "Triple Bottom Line: A business metaphor for a social construct." Portland State University, School of Business Administration(2006)
[23] See: Quadruple Bottom Line Reporting | eHow.com
http://www.ehow.com/about_5229554_quadruple-bottom-line-reporting.html#ixzz1jZ6bqTLZ

commitment of a business to protect the environment by recycling or investing in a community project to protect a river? Meanwhile there is a growing literature showing how responsible or sustainable business practices affect a company's financial results. [24]

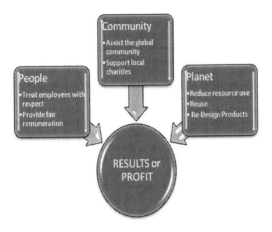

FIGURE 2.2 Components Of A Good Company

Figure 2.2 Components of a Good Company, expands on just how the parts to the good company system fit together, combining to contribute to the company's financial sustainability or profit. This is in direct contrast to traditional models which view investments in socially responsible actions as coming at the expense of profits.

Good Companies Empower People

A good company honors its employees by rewarding them fairly and giving them the freedom to solve problems and find creative solutions. Although a good company earns fair returns for shareholders, it refuses to do so at the expense of the legitimate interests of other stakeholders. An organization which is perceived as generous builds trust and confidence among customers, employees, and the public.

Semco Group, a Brazilian company that leads the market in industrial equipment and solutions for document management, embodies an

---

[24] See: Disadvantages of Triple Bottom Line Reporting | eHow.com
http://www.ehow.com/info_8509816_disadvantages-triple-bottom-line-reporting.html#ixzz1jZ7pDsLp

employee-first, positive value system. Semco's Chairman Ricardo Semler encourages employees to suggest what they should be paid, to evaluate their supervisors, to learn each other's jobs, and to tolerate dissent, even when divisive. To enable transparency, Semler devised a profit-sharing system and insisted that the company's financial statements be published internally. His good company treatment of employees paid off: Semco's revenues jumped from $1 million to over $300 million between 1980 and 2010. And the firm grew from several hundred employees to 3,000, with a remarkably low turnover of about one percent. From a base of manufacturing appliances, Semco also expanded into providing outsourced management services for several of Brazil's biggest banks, as well as environmental site remediation and risk management services. You will read more about Semco later.

How does respecting employees and treating them fairly produce such remarkable results? Globe Scan, a public opinion and business intelligence organization, found that the fair treatment of employees was the most important indicator of company success in the 26 countries surveyed, including the US, France, Switzerland, Italy, the Philippines, and all of Latin America.

Good Companies Support And Engage The Community

Beyond treating employees fairly, a good company is also committed to working with and supporting the community. Some support the community by providing donations and publicity for community events. Others provide financial support for non-profits and the arts. Some firms, like Dansko Shoes and Google, have established foundations that support a variety of causes and community development efforts. Others, like RSF Social Finance and Triodos Bank, directly finance community development. Give Something Back gives a portion of its annual profits away, while Proctor and Gamble pays for employees' time spent working for charities.

Give Something Back, an office products supplier founded in 1991 by partners Mike Hannigan and Sean Marx, has given away over $4 million, or 78 percent of its profits to about 500 community organizations working on a range of issues. "Our principal stakeholder is the community," explains

Hannigan, who says that the firm's resources are best used when going into making the community a better, safer, more productive place. "We sell goods which earn revenue and generate profits in the marketplace, and then we let the community decide where those dollars are needed," he says.

Apple Computer is another firm that has indirectly given back to the community; in developing the personal computer, Steve Jobs joined a group of employees and investors to develop a product that has improved communications on a global scale. Think about it: today, thanks to Apple's early work, farmers in rural India now use telecommunications and computers to access weather, crop, and price information vastly improving the incomes of their communities.[25]

Good Companies Serve The Global Community

Growing numbers of global citizens, people who see themselves as part of a global community, are coming to realize that the decisions of companies at home and abroad affect other people around the world for better and for worse. Apple Computer suffered a major setback to its shining reputation due to the public outcry over a wave of suicides at one of its largest subcontractors, Foxconn, located in Shenzhen, China in 2011. Apple's Supplier Responsibility Report, an audit of the company's 127 subcontract facilities, pointed to the harsh working conditions in these factories, an issue the company hopes to address by joining the Fair Labor Association. The FLA was established in 1999 to monitor global workplaces. Apple's decision to join FLA highlights the risks to global companies that outsource production in order to cut costs. [26]

While globalization has benefited some, it has been accompanied by increasing consumer concern over the environmental, health and economic conditions around the world. Consumers want to know: Are companies treating their workers fairly? Are workers being compensated fairly? Do the

---

[25] see C.K. Prahalad. The Fortune at the Bottom of the Pyramid.Wharton School Publishing. 2005 pp.319-358

[26] www.bloomberg.com/news/2012-01-13/apple-opens-suppliers-doors-to-labor-group-after-foxconn-worker-suicides.html

products we buy contain harmful chemicals? Is the workplace safe? And are environmental practices affecting my health?

And there is genuine cause for concern. Consider some facts:

- Globally, 850 million people earn less than a living wage. [27]

- Some 250 million child laborers, between the ages of 4 and 14, toil daily just to survive.[28]

- El Salvadorans earning minimum wage bring home 60 cents per hour; they need at least $1.73 per hour to pull themselves out of poverty.[29]

- Only 12 percent of the price of your jeans goes to the Honduran and Cambodian workers who made them.[30]

- Only 10 percent of the price of your espresso or cappuccino went to the grower. [31]

These are some of the byproducts of a world in which the wealthiest 15 percent of the population consumes 75 percent of the world's resources. More and more, companies are considering their global impact and some are building service to the global community into their company DNA or mission statement. A growing number of enterprises are successfully meeting the needs of the underserved community. It would be easy for companies to ignore these problems, but a good company chooses to face the social challenge.

For example, meeting the health needs of millions who are underserved and ignored often requires that companies redesign their products, their

---

[27] http://www.humanitycampaign.org/global-poverty-facts/

[28] http://filipspagnoli.wordpress.com/stats-on-human-rights/statistics-on-labor-conditions/statistics-on-child-labor/

[29] This information comes from William Young and Richard Welford. Ethical Shopper. Fusion Press. London 2002

[30] UNITE, the Union of Needletrades, Industrial and Textile Employees

[31] In contrast, the Kuapa Kokoo Fair Trade chocolate cooperative is owned by 45,000 Ghanaian farmers. While world cocoa prices have fallen to around $1000 per ton, Kuapa Kokoo receives a guaranteed, stable Fair Trade price of $1,600 per ton plus a $150 per ton premium. That premium has helped fund community projects, a credit union for farmers, cash bonuses and efforts to enhance the status and participation of local women.

design, or their methods of delivering their products or services to those in need. In India each year, tens of thousands of people die from kala-azar, the black fever. This fatal disease is spread by sand flies that bite people as they sleep. Few can afford the expensive cure. When executives of OneWorldHealth heard about a decades-old antibiotic, they tested it and developed a full course of treatment for as little as $10. OneWorldHealth, the world's first non-profit pharmaceutical company, defines its mission as providing affordable treatments of infectious diseases to the world's poor. Founded in 2000 by Dr. Victoria Hale, the company finds new uses for existing medicines and identifies promising medicines that have been abandoned by drug companies as unprofitable. "Ninety percent of pharmaceutical research money goes to the diseases that affect only ten percent of the people," says Nina Grove, OneWorldHealth's vice-president for access and delivery. Julie Cheng, vice president and general counsel adds "There are lots of perfectly fine drugs or drug candidates that get discarded because the people who are developing them don't see the potential for a high-value market." In an innovative agreement with the pharmaceutical giant Roche, OneWorldHealth has been granted access to use Roche's vast proprietary library of drug compounds as a research resource for future innovations to serve the unmet health needs of the poor..

As a retail store, Baksheesh Fair Trade is a for-profit business with a non-profit mission. It imports products from approximately 40 different countries, through approximately 27 different retailers. Baksheesh's mission is very straightforward: to grow Fair Trade as much as possible while adhering to the highest standards of ethical business. The principles of fair trade are closely followed through this mission and are met each day, with each transaction. These nine principles include (a) paying a fair wage promptly, (b) providing opportunities for economically and socially marginalized producers, (c) developing transparent and accountable relationships, (d) building capacity, (e) supporting safe working conditions, (f) ensuring the rights of children, (g) cultivating environmental stewardship and (h) respecting cultural identity. Baksheesh accomplishes this by buying, selling and promoting fair trade products. Their relationships with wholesalers and artisan groups are based on these strong values, and they are always upheld. [32]

Good Companies Care For The Planet

The earth produces in abundance all the resources needed to sustain life for most of its inhabitants. Starting with the industrial revolution, we have developed a global powerhouse based on energy, machines, and technology. Unfortunately, these advances have come at great cost. Today, our planet is embroiled in a struggle with resources and pollution. Lester Brown, President of the Earth Policy Institute, reminds us of where our focus must be: "Our global economy is outgrowing the capacity of the earth to support it," he said. "In our preoccupation with quarterly earnings reports and year-to-year economic growth, we have lost sight of how large the human enterprise has become relative to the earth's resources ... As a result, we are consuming renewable resources faster than they can regenerate." [33]

A good company is conscious of the sources of all raw materials and its environmental footprint on the planet. Its practices are designed to steward the earth's resources, limiting and reducing toxic emissions in our water and air while working toward replacing non-renewable resources with regenerative materials. It may implement measures to reduce, prevent or eliminate environmental impacts such as reducing waste or redesigning production processes to conserve energy and raw materials. Clif Bar supports a broad range of programs and activities in an effort to reduce the company's ecological footprint. These range from auditing and modifying its supply chain to finding products that are produced with organic or sustainable methods.

Ray Anderson, former CEO of Interface Carpets, changed his company's trajectory after customers began asking hard questions about what Interface was doing for the environment, questions that neither he nor his staff could answer. "I [had] never given a thought of what we were taking from the earth, doing to the earth, to make our products, as long as there's enough of

---

[32] Emily Poisson. Bakheesh Fair Trade Case Study. May 2011.
[33] Lester Brown. Plan B 2.0. Norton 2006 p. 3

that stuff running through the pipe lines to keep the factories running," he explained.

Anderson organized a task force of representatives from the company's businesses around the world and challenged the research group to figure out what the company could do. What emerged was a series of steps to cut its resource use and use fewer supplies, reuse where possible, reclaim resources, recycle, redesign products, adopt best practices, and challenge suppliers to do the same. Interface also launched a new effort to keep carpet out of the landfill. Called Evergreen Service Contracts, it allows customers to lease carpet which is then recycled by the company.

Interface's sales increased 63 percent as a result of its efforts, and profits doubled. Interface's ambitious plan to transform itself within a heavily petrochemical-dependent industry like carpeting shows that not only can such moves reduce the footprint; it can also boost profits.

Just 40 miles north of San Francisco on the site of an abandoned electronics factory, Brad Baker, CEO of Codding Enterprises is building North America's first One Planet Community, a network of the world's greenest neighborhoods. Baker's commitment to the environment is helping to transform the economy of Sonoma County, while serving as a model for the world. Using as his template Figure 2.3 One Planet Community Guidelines (see below), Baker is designing a 21st Century community.[34] Sonoma Mountain Village, the first One Planet Community in the US, will meet the needs of the community's 200 units with state of the art green technology and features like renewable energy, passive solar heating and measures to provide for zero waste and recycled water. They installed a 1.2 megawatt solar array producing enough electricity to power 540 homes, a geothermal heat exchanger that can be used for both heating and cooling (doing away with the need for separate furnace and air-conditioning systems while supplying free hot water heating during the summer months) and a rainwater collection system. They also enabled energy savings with lighting retrofits and the installation of lighting timers in the commercial areas. To address social sustainability, the village will offer on-site jobs, community

---

[34] http://www.oneplanetcommunities.org/communities/endorsed-communities/sonoma-mountain-village/

gardens and wetlands restoration. Baker is still in the early stages on his path to building a new sustainable community. But, he is well on his way. Already, he has enlisted nearly 40 businesses, including Comcast and Azonde Corporation (manufacturers of solar powered wireless water monitor systems), to form the commercial base of the community.

Zero carbon	making buildings more energy efficient and delivering all energy with renewable technologies
Zero waste	reducing waste, reusing where possible, and ultimately sending zero waste to landfill
Sustainable transport	encouraging low carbon modes of transport to reduce emissions, reducing the need to travel
Sustainable materials	using sustainable and healthy products, such as those with low embodied energy, sourced locally, made from renewable or waste resources
Local and sustainable food	choosing low impact, local, seasonal and organic diets and reducing food waste
Sustainable water	using water more efficiently in buildings and in the products we buy; tackling local flooding and water course pollution
Land use and wildlife	protecting and restoring existing biodiversity and natural habitats through appropriate land use and integration into the built environment
Culture and heritage	reviving local identity and wisdom; supporting and participating in the arts
Equity and local economy	creating bioregional economies that support fair employment, inclusive communities and international fair trade
Health and happiness	encouraging active, sociable, meaningful lives to promote good health and well being

FIGURE 2.3 One-Planet Community Guidelines

In Brazil, Natura Cosmeticos faces a different set of issues. Brazil's rich biodiversity is the source of its raw materials. Millions of people depend on the land for their livelihoods. In order to ensure that ingredients derived from Brazilian flora are harvested using socially and environmentally sound practices, Natura Cosmeticos designed a Program for Certification of Suppliers. The program is designed to promote sustainable practices for the extraction of raw materials. In addition, Natura is educating indigenous communities about the importance of diversifying the products they farm and supporting local conservation efforts. Indigenous communities are gaining skills, an understanding of sustainable economic practices relating to bio-diverse genetic resources, and new economic opportunities with Natura that contribute to greater economic stability in their communities.

Good Companies Do Well

When companies treat people fairly, care for the community and protect the environment, they can reap the rewards of reduced expenses and an enhanced reputation. Authors Daniel Esty and Andrew Winston in their book Green to Gold say it well:

"Efforts to cut waste and reduce resource use, often called 'eco-efficiency,' can save money that drops almost immediately to the bottom line. Redesign a process to use less energy, and you'll lower your exposure to volatile oil and gas prices. Redesign your product so it doesn't have toxic substances, and you'll cut regulatory burdens—and perhaps avoid a value-destroying incident down the road. These efforts lower business risk while protecting the gold—reliable cash flows, brand value and customer loyalty, for example—that companies have painstakingly collected over time."[35]

Esty and Winston also provide numerous examples of good companies reaping financial benefits, including the chemical giant DuPont, which cut its greenhouse gas emissions by 72 percent and held its energy use constant. "Through constant vigilance and innovation, the company found a hundred ways to get leaner and meet its energy target," write the authors. "Over the past decade, this strategy has saved DuPont $2 billion." Similarly, 3M's program, Pollution Prevention Pays, which encourages employees to propose waste-cutting, money-saving ideas, led to cuts of 2.6 billion pounds of pollutants and saved the company an estimated $1 billion.[12] Business

---

[35] Daniel Esty and Andre Winston. Green to Gold. Wiley 2006 p. 13

consultant Hunter Lovins adds "DuPont became a company that's profitable because its protecting the climate." [36]

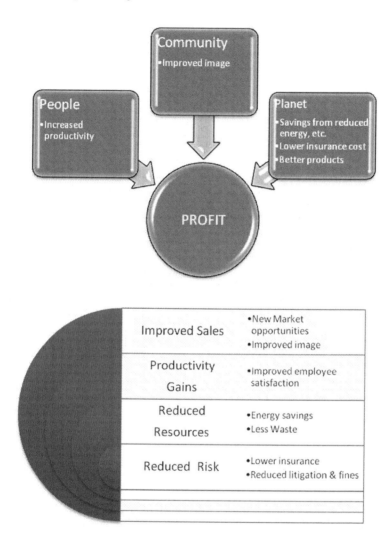

FIGURE 2.4: How Good Companies Produces Results

[36] Esty and Winston p. 105-107; Hunter Lovins and Boyd Cohen. Climate Capitalism. Hill and Wang.2011 p7

Figure 2.4 illustrates just how a company's values and its attention to people and the environment can produce results. Gains occur in the form of improved sales and productivity as new market opportunities are uncovered and customers connect with the improved image. As the company prioritizes human relationships, employees become more satisfied and their productivity increases. In addition, companies gain from reduced risk exposure saving money from reduced insurance rates, less litigation and fewer fines. Good companies also save from lower utility and disposal costs.[37]

Corporate financiers are seeing the financial connection. A report in CFO Magazine noted that Wal-Mart "discovered that by packaging just one of the company's own products in smaller boxes, [it] could dramatically cut down its distribution and shipping costs, reducing energy use at the same time. Such realizations have driven the company's re-examination of its packaging and fleet efficiency." [38]

Edward Nusbaum, CEO of the global accounting firm Grant Thornton, reported in an interview with CFO Magazine that his firm saw a four percent drop in employee turnover, a drop he attributed to the company's increased focus on community outreach, fundraising, and company-approved community volunteerism. "Every percentage point that we increase our retention saves so many millions of dollars in training," he explained. "But it's as important that these events increase employees' passion for the firm. A positive experience for employees translates to a positive experience for clients." GE's CFO Jim Lawrence agreed. "It's not social responsibility versus profitability," he said. "It's social responsibility

---

[37] While in general this model is a good predictor of success; it is not by any means a guarantee since so many market variable will affect a company's profitability. And there is the example of Nau, outdoor apparel clothing company, founded 2005 and based in Portland, Oregon, which did all the right things in terms of support to the community and designing its material from the most planet friendly materials and went bankrupt. In part its failure was due to the recession of 2008 but also because of its overly ambitious and unrealistic business plan. On May 2, 2008, Nau announced that it was ceasing operations, primarily due to an inability to raise further capital. The company was later bought out and continued its "green" mission includes the use of textiles developed from high quality sustainable technical fibers Nau's core "social" mission involves a donation of 2% from each sale to selected community partners chosen by the customer upon purchase. While information about its profitability is not available, the company has been operating successfully since 2010..

[38] Kate O'Sullivan. "Virtue Rewarded" CFO; October 2006 p. 48

and profitability." Beth Nickels, finance chief at Herman Miller, an office furniture manufacturer, also shared that her company "sees $4.5 million in annual savings from $2 million in annual spending on environmental initiatives."[39]

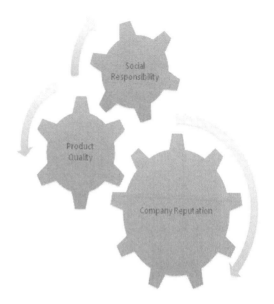

FIGURE 2.5 Drivers Of A Company's Reputation

Figures 2.5 illustrates just how a company's reputation is driven by the quality of its products and its social responsibility. Working in conjunction, these are the elements of the company's financial performance.

In its Global Sustainability Report, Price-Waterhouse-Coopers suggests that sustainability is not just desirable, but also required in today's corporate environment.

"Sustainability may sound like yet another corporate buzz word, the latest fad in a long line of management fads. But sustainability is serious business. A new standard of performance that measures the social, environmental, and economic effects of business activities—the so-called "triple bottom line"—it can mean the difference between a company's long-term success and failure. Few corporations recognize the links between sustainability,

---
[39] Kate O'Sullivan. "Virtue Rewarded" CFO; October 2006 p. 51-52

36

reputation, and financial performance. However, without a sustainability risk management program in place, companies are flirting with disaster. A major misstep or miscalculation on triple-bottom-line issues can ruin reputations, jeopardize corporate financial integrity, and imperil relationships with customers, investors, and the banks." [40]

Research shows that responsible practices not only benefit society, but also make companies profitable. Reviewing the stock market performance of large U.S. manufacturing companies, Irene Herremans, Parporn Akathaporn, and Morris McInnes concluded that companies that serve the community and protect the planet outperformed peer companies while they "provided investors better stock market returns and lower risk." [41]

In another study of 67 large US corporations titled "The Corporate Social-financial Performance Relationship," Lee Preston and Douglas O'Bannon concluded that evidence indicates "there is a positive association between social and financial performance." [42]

Laurie Bassi, Ed Frauenheim and Dan McMurrer created the Good Company Index to take a systematic look at the records of Fortune 100 companies as employers, sellers and stewards of society and the planet. What they found was that companies with higher scores on their index outperformed their peers in the stock market. [43]

More than 50 academic studies on the financial impact of social responsibility when taken together showed that companies that gave back to the community and protected the environment improved their financial performance. Some 33 studies showed a clear positive relationship while only five studies indicated a negative relationship. The authors concluded that "the vast majority of studies support the idea that, at the very least,

---

[40] www.pwc.co.uk/annualreport08/

[41] Irene M. Herremans,Parporn Akathaporn,Morris McInnes "An investigation of corporate social responsibility reputation and economic performance" Accounting, Organizations and Society; Volume 18, Issues 7-8, October- November 1993, Pages 587-604

[42] Business and Society; v.36 n. 4, December 1997. P. 426

[43] Good Company: Business Success in the Worthiness Era; Berrett-Koehler; 2011

good social performance does not lead to poor financial performance, Indeed, most of the studies reviewed indicate a positive correlation."[44]

According to the 2010 Ethisphere Media Responsibility Report, companies which pursue high ethical standards benefit even in a recession. Figure 2.6 compares the "WME Index," of the 100 leading publicly traded 2010 World's Most Ethical Companies, against the US stock market index S&P 500 and UK's index FTSE since 2005.[45]

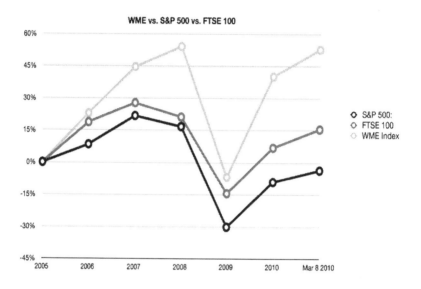

Figure 2.6 The World's Most Ethical Companies Outperform US and UK Stock Market Indexes

The U.N. Global Compact encourages businesses to pay closer attention to the social impact of their business conduct. In order to assess how effectively companies are improving human rights, labor standards, protecting the environment and standing firm against corruption, the U.N. is reaching out to specialists around the world using collaborative software to enable them to review and comment on the progress of each company

---

[44] see: Ronald Roman, Sefa Hayibor and Bradley Agle, The Relationship between Social and Financial Performance. Business and Society. V 38 n 1 March 1999. Pp. 109-125.
[45] http://ethisphere.com/past-wme-honorees/wme2010/

and review the evidence of commitment and action on each of the ten principles. The Global Compact provides a network so that companies can share ideas about corporate citizenship. And while it has become an important driver of social responsibility, these are merely guidelines for how companies should behave. There is still no standard system of accountability for evaluating and measuring a company's ethical performance.

However, this is starting to change. B-Lab, the organization which certifies Beneficial Corporations, has developed a comprehensive rating system that assesses a company's policies and actions. The rating system is based on responses to more than 200 questions about a company's policies, business practices and strategy. It measures the company's performance with respect to a quintuple bottom-lime: (1) accountability and governance, (2) employee compensation and workplace environment, (3) consumer benefit, (4) community sourcing and charity, and (5) the environment. The B-Lab rating system is discussed in greater detail in the concluding chapter.

Many of the companies discussed in this book are working to combine transparent governance, respect for employees and the community, and sustainable technologies to support global security by promoting equity, justice, and human welfare. By attempting to balance the needs of all stakeholders, good companies promote the creation of a better world.

CHAPTER 3

GIVE SOMETHING BACK

Give Something Back (GSB) is an office products company located in a gritty industrial area in Oakland, California. Founded in 1991 by Mike Hannigan and Sean Marx, GSB is a company that does good and is considered by its employees as the best place to work in America. GSB is also California's largest independent office products company with corporate offices in three cities and 12,000 clients and 40 distribution centers nationwide, but it is best known for donating a large share of company profits. Since formation, the company has given away nearly $5 million, or 78 percent of its profits, to about 500 community organizations working on a host of issues.

Doing good has paid for this company: GSB was named by INC Magazine as one of the fastest growing businesses in America three years in a row beginning in 1999.[46] When the financial meltdown hit in 2008, while competitor Office Depot sold its New York real estate to raise revenue to finance daily operations, GSB sailed through the crisis, having anticipated its financial needs and being able to rely on the goodwill it accumulated over its two-decade history.

It could be said that the company was born, quite literally, over a plate of spaghetti. Several nights a week, Hannigan fixed spaghetti for dinner,

---

[46] www.gsb.com

pouring Newman's Own spaghetti sauce over the noodles and onto his plate. "I started reading the label. I discovered that I was getting the product I wanted without making any financial sacrifice, and the profits from my purchase went to a national charity," he explained.[47]

GSB's Business Model

In evaluating GSB in the light of other good companies, the firm stands out through its combination of values, virtues, and sales volume. "As a business, our competitive advantage is selling at the lowest price," said Hannigan, who, with Marx, started out in business by selling copiers. When a conglomerate gobbled up the company they worked for, the pair thought about building a business that served the community. "We were aware of Newman's Own," said Hannigan. "We knew that they had a good product that was competitively priced; consumers got what they wanted; and the profits were donated to support a children's charity. Well, I wasn't sure how successful we would be since I don't exactly look like Paul Newman," he quipped, "but, still, we thought, we could give it a try, too."[48]

Hannigan explains the company's business model "Every successful business gives their profits away. Eventually the profits go out as dividends or appreciated stock to the owners. The main difference with us is that we give the money away to organizations that are connected to the well being of the community. And it's not because we want to, it's because everyone wants to. We have a business model that facilitates what everyone would choose to do in the first place; we just make it easy and free of sacrifice. Eighty to ninety percent of consumers say, "If you can prove it doesn't cost any more and it benefits my community, I'll buy from you." By choosing us instead of another supplier, our customers have the opportunity to help others. That gives us stickiness with our customers that I think other companies don't have. We have better customer retention than Staples, for example."[49]

---

[47] Presentation to Sonoma State University EMBA Cohort 1. March 5, 2011.
[48] Presentation to Sonoma State University EMBA Cohort 1. March 5, 2011.
[49] The Paul Newman Way to Buy Office Supplies: The Give Something Back Story
http://causecapitalism.com/the- paul-newman-way-to-buy-office-supplies-the-give-something-back-story/#more-4

Giving back to the Community

Each day, GSB's staff takes orders for office supplies and furniture from business accounts over the phone and Internet; each night suppliers deliver ordered goods to an empty warehouse. The next day, trucks load the goods and deliver orders to customers. In most businesses, the profits from such a venture would go to the owners and investors, but not at GSB. "Heck, all we are doing," said Hannigan, with the self-deprecating humor he is known for, "is eliminating the interests of the stockholders and moving those profits directly into the community. We're just like Office Depot, except they are a $16 billion company and we're $30 million."[50]

Emulating Paul Newman's model, Hannigan and Marx committed to paying themselves a reasonable salary and giving profits to the community. During a presentation to a cohort of MBA students at Sonoma State University, Hannigan, with uncharacteristic seriousness, explained what they do, and why. "We are the richest country in the world but 43 million people lack basic health care and our public schools are failing," he said. "How can that be? As a business we felt that we just had to do something to change that."

And make change, they have, thanks not only to a plate of spaghetti, but also to the proceeds from an insurance payout. "Our business started with $40,000" Hannigan said. "We could have donated the money; Sean and I could have each donated $20,000 to a food bank, but we didn't. We invested it into a business and with that $40,000 we've produced millions of dollars in donations and given hundreds of people jobs. That's the power of business; translating a modest investment into this giant benefit."[51]

"Who benefits? Everyone: GSB's founders, suppliers, customers, employees, and especially", said Hannigan, "the community."

GSB sees its principal stakeholder as the community. The company earns revenue and generates profits in the marketplace and then lets the community decide where those dollars are most needed. Hannigan adds "We put our resources into making the community a better, safer, more productive place.

---

[50] Presentation to Sonoma State University EMBA Cohort 1. March 5, 2011

[51] Bernice Yeung."Taking Care of Customers to help the Community." East Bay Express May 26-June 1, 2010. Pp. 34-35.

We trust our employees and we trust the community. I feel that if we put our resources under the democratic control of our employees together with the community, they will act in their best interests."[52]

GSB decides where to give its donations by asking employees, customers, and even customers' employees to vote. "Each year we send out a ballot asking our customers to tell us where we should donate our profits," said Hannigan.

With votes counted and decisions made, the firm then hosts a party during which much of the year's profits are given away. The annual event, held in the Oakland Rotunda, an elegant arcade in the city's center, is always replete with local jazz bands and Napa Valley wine. One by one, GSB's employees come to the stage to present cash awards to organizations ranging from the Blind Babies Foundation and Habitat for Humanity to My Red Shoes, The Rabbit Haven, and PAWS. My Red Shoes gives clothing to impoverished families, while PAWS advocates for animals by operating a companion animal shelter, a wildlife center, and an advocacy department. "You'd be surprised at how much we give to every kind of activity," said Hannigan. "Some of my employees want to give it all to care for animals. And I like animals; I had a tasty one for dinner," he joked.

Greening the Company

At one recent event, after the festivities had ended, after the last check had been handed out, CEO Sean Marx took to the stage to close the gathering—with his face painted green. His soliloquy illustrated that the company cares not only for its community, but also for the planet as a whole.

"I'll bet you are all wondering why my face is green. Well the paper industry is the fourth largest producer of greenhouse gases. Paper is our number one product. Because we consume so much paper, our forests are only one-tenth of what they were. Our number two item is toner; over one-half of the toner cartridges end up in landfill. So what are we doing about this? That's why my face is green—GSB has been going green since day one. Over 85 percent of the paper we sell is recycled versus only 10 percent for our competitors. We have a responsibility to green this industry. What does

---

[52] Presentation to Sonoma State University EMBA Cohort 2, Dec 11, 2011.

that mean? First we are a certified green business and we are helping our customers to go green themselves. To help them we have added a "green-it" feature to our website. When a customer attempts to buy a non-recyclable product—a pop-up alerts them and offers several green alternatives. We want to make it easy for our customers to go green."

More green is yet on the way: GSB has also added 75,000 watts in solar panels to its rooftop and is planning to replace its delivery fleet with bio-diesel and hybrid vehicles.[53]

GSB also seeks sustainability, as is illustrated by its agreement with the paper distributor Boise to donate $1 to a food bank for each carton of paper it sells. Beyond this GSB also seeks to reduce waste and increase efficiency whenever and wherever possible. "We wondered how we could use our trucks more effectively," shared CEO Marx. "We send them out full and they come back empty. Well, electronic waste can be recycled." Now, when GSB drivers drop off merchandise they pick up empty boxes and e-waste. Hannigan and Marx consider making GSB green and sustainable as part of their service to the community. The pair hired Stephanie Schlect to act as the firm's Sustainability Coordinator, a role designed to keep GSB moving along the good path.

A Good Place to Work

Give Something Back is also a good place to work, encouraging employees to participate in social projects and volunteer opportunities. On any given day, you are likely to find GSB employees sitting on nonprofit boards, donating talents and skills to community efforts, and mentoring disadvantaged youth. Alma Azarcon, director of Human Resources, has been working for ten years at *Give Something Back*; her passion is for a social activity in Oakland and the larger Bay Area called "Rebuilding Together," which brings volunteers together to upgrade the homes of the low income elderly and community centers. Tracey Bowers, sales manager at the firm's Sacramento, California office appreciates the giving culture at GSB. "I have worked all over at lots of different companies," she said. "But GSB is like my

---

[53] Presentation to Sonoma State University EMBA Cohort 1. March 5, 2011.

home. I wouldn't work any place else." Another employee, Shirley Meredith, agreed. "I get up every morning with a smile," she said. "Mike [Hannigan] makes coming to work so much fun." Employees see Hannigan as a zany cheerleader with degrees in philosophy and criminology who spends his days circulating in the open office space entertaining everyone with his sharp wit.

GSB's culture is not a secret; the company was nominated by INC Magazine as the best place to work in the US. Beyond encouraging volunteerism and just having a good time, Hannigan explained why.

"We pay the full premiums on health care for our employees. We feel it's a human right. Some competitors cut health care to keep their stocks competitive, but we made the decision based on a different kind of stakeholder. We are growing people, hiring them from youth employment partnerships, economic stimulus programs. We are bringing people in and growing them and advancing them....and the employees participate in the distribution of profits."[54]

Hannigan, as seems to be true of the founders of other Good Companies, believes that the future of both people and planet depends on the actions of businesses like his.

"Many people are still surprised that a business might have anything in mind other than the bottom line, but that tradition is changing. There's a much greater openness among business consumers to incorporate social and environmental criteria into their decision making process. Professional purchasers are asking about the environmental impact of a vendor's products and about the way they treat their workers. And vendors, to their credit, are incorporating these issues into the way they do business. That's not because they woke up one morning and decided to 'make a difference'; it's because their corporate customers are demanding it."

---

[54] Bernice Yeung."Taking Care of Customers to help the Community." East Bay Express May 26-June 1, 2010. Pp. 34-35.

CHAPTER 4

VESTERGAARD FRANDSEN

"The things we most avidly wish for—universal love, perfect justice, untainted goodness—we cannot achieve. But if we stopped working for them we would be lesser creatures."

JEDEDIAH PURDY, FOR COMMON THINGS

What transforms a modest, Danish manufacturer of hotel and restaurant uniforms into a global, humanitarian leader in the fights against malaria, diahhreal disease and AIDS? In the case of Vestergaard Frandsen, S.A., it was a young Dane's firsthand experience with heartbreaking poverty as an entrepreneur in Africa at the age of 19.

With little interest in joining his family's textile firm, which launched in 1957 and eventually tapped a growing market for women's clothing, the young Mikkel Vestergaard-Frandsen chose to leave his native Denmark after graduating from high school, seeking adventure by backpacking through India and Africa. "This experience ignited my passion for Africa and guided a strategic overhaul of our family textile business into a dynamic force, driving positive change in preventing malaria, guinea worm, diarrhea, HIV and more."

"I started out as an entrepreneur in Africa, where at the age of 19 I opened my first company in Lagos," explained Vestergaard Frandsen, the grandson of the original firm's founder. While in Nigeria, Mikkel also discovered there was opportunity in Africa for textiles, which he began importing into Lagos from Denmark. "I was flying home and picking up secondhand clothes and then flying back and selling them off before they went through customs," he explained during an interview with Adweek. "I did that so I didn't have to deal with Nigerian authorities, and the client would then have them cleared."[55]

When he finally returned to Denmark, Vestergaard Frandsen, led at the time by Mikkel's father Torben, struck a deal to buy a million yards of old wool from Sweden's civil defense stockpiles. As Mikkel put it "Going to Africa the first time had a lot more to do with adventure than business, and... it really gave me, personally, a heartbeat and something that was worth fighting for and working for. I could not see myself doing textiles for the Scandinavian market, so we struck a deal that I could get involved exporting textiles to Africa."[56]

Father and son determined to cut the wool into blankets and to sell those blankets to the Red Cross for distribution to refugees in Rwanda and Kurdistan. Mikkel and his father seized this new business opportunity and began exporting textiles for distribution in the third world. The company's fabric and textile expertise quickly positioned Vestergaard Frandsen as the frontrunner in the field, and by the mid 1990s, the side venture had outpaced and outperformed the family uniform business, eventually replacing it altogether.

Dedicated to Improve World Health

Exporting textiles to the third world was profitable. Sleeping sickness is spread by horseflies and with one bite they can put the victim into a coma. Years of fabric and textile experience gave Vestergaard-Frandsen the ability to produce blankets that repelled the horsefly and malaria carrying mosquitos. Malaria was eradicated in the US over fifty years ago, but in Africa it kills 3,000 children every day. Elisabeth Wilhelm, Vestergaard Frandsen's public relations specialist says "There is no reason a child born

---

[55]http://www.adweek.com/aw/content_display/creative/features/e3ie188ab48abcdb04998cf19a98a69e688 retrieved 09 January 2011.
[56] http://www.youtube.com/watch?v=1bjBxo0mkJw

in the year 2010 should die from malaria and the fact that this continues to happen is completely unacceptable."[57] There are approximately 300 million cases of malaria worldwide each year causing more than a million deaths. Malaria costs Africa over $12 billion annually in lost productivity and its treatment consumes some 40 percent of hospital expenditures.[58]

Mikkel subsequently moved to Nairobi, where he began distributing mosquito nets in 1994, at first sourcing them out of Thailand. In 1997 with revenues at $5.5 million, Mikkel and his father Torben agreed to set up two parallel businesses; Torben would continue with the uniform business while Mikkel would focus exclusively on humanitarian textiles. Gradually Mikkel bought out his father's company, dropped the uniform business and brought in professional managers.[59]

Before long, however, lower-cost Indian, Pakistani and Chinese manufacturers made it difficult for Vestergaard Frandsen to compete. The firm faced a choice: cut costs or increase quality. "Everybody else was picking the cost-leadership route," Mikkel told the Financial Times, leading him to move in the opposite direction and to differentiate instead by investing heavily in research and development and by licensing producers in Vietnam, where the firm's nets, called PermaNet®, are still made. [60] By 2005, the company's factories in Vietnam and Thailand were producing two million PermaNet® each month to be sold to relief and development agencies that distribute them free or at highly subsidized rates mainly in Africa.[61] But by 2010, with a change in the company's strategy, that number had skyrocketed to over 100 million.[62]

The firm had also been researching ways to produce clothes from fabric that did not fade in sunlight and did not weaken when permeated with the insecticide needed to protect wearers from the deadly horsefly that carries

[57] Rob Jones and John Sullivan. Vestergaard-Frandsen:Case Study. May 19,2010. P.2.

[58] www.malarianomore.org/about. Retrieved May 14, 2010.

[59] Freedman, Michael. "A Fine Mesh." Forbes.com. December 26, 2005.
http://www.forbes.com/forbes/2005/1226/071.html

[60] http://www.nextbillion.net/news/a-responsible-profit-from-the-war-on-malaria retrieved 08 January 2011.

[61] Freedman, Michael. "A Fine Mesh." Forbes.com. December 26, 2005.
http://www.forbes.com/forbes/2005/1226/071.html

[62] Sanne Fournier-Wendes personal interview. Lausanne, Switzerland June 24, 2011.

sleeping sickness in Africa. The solution turned out to be ZeroFly®, a durable plastic sheeting for sheltering refugees, which also kills disease-spreading insects. And recently it added ZeroVector® durable lining and PermaNet® 3.0 with increased efficacy against insecticide-resistant mosquitos.

Vestergaard Frandsen then developed a low-cost water filtering system that, using hollow-fiber membrane technology, packs a water filter into a short plastic pipe the size of a paper towel cylinder to eliminate bacteria, parasites and some viruses.[63] That water filter, called LifeStraw®, now serves villages in Latin America, Africa and Asia that lack safe drinking water. It also transformed Vestergaard Frandsen's product line, which now includes a larger version of the water filter called LifeStraw® Family that filters twelve liters an hour and lasts a family of five for at least three years. LifeStraw® is a revolutionary water filtration plant in a straw that takes out all unwanted particles and 99.9999% of all bacteria. Mikkel adds "LifeStraw® has the potential to create a life without the preventable water-born diseases that today, claim 6,000 children every day. "[64]

An Innovative Business Model

Vestergaard Frandsen's products are sold in mass quantities to nonprofit, philanthropic, governmental and religious organizations.[65] Sanne Fournier-Wendes is Vestergaard Frandsen's Global Partnership Manager and is responsible for coordinating partnerships with a range of international organizations such as the Global Fund for HIV/AIDS, TB and Malaria and the World Health Organization to fulfill the company's mission:. "Vestergaard Frandsen's innovation in disease control textiles is fueled by our humanitarian entrepreneurship to create a healthier planet." "Global health is all about

---

[63] LifeStraw was first developed by Vestergaard-Frandsen to filter out the guinea worm larvae. With the widespread use of LifeStraw the Carter Center has predicted that guinea worm disease "will be the first parasitic disease to be eradicated and the first disease to be eradicated without the use of vaccines or medical treatment". In 1986, there were an estimated 3.5 million cases of Guinea worm in 20 endemic nations in Asia and Africa.[6] The number of cases has been reduced by more than 99% to just 1785 cases in 2010 according to the Carter Center.

[64] http://www.youtube.com/watch?v=1bjBxo0mkJw

[65] Realizing that it would need to reduce costs and find new distribution channels when aid money dried up, the firm sought to reach end-users directly through traditional retail markets and briefly experimented with the sale of PermaNet 3.0 at gas stations for about $4.

partnerships between the public sector, non- governmental organizations and the private sector." She adds Vestergaard-Frandsen plays a crucial role in this equation by constantly innovating and developing new products. We play a proactive role by finding new ways to solve challenging health problems."[66]

As Vestergaard Frandsen evolved from a high quality, low-cost manufacturer of textiles to a world leader in the fight against malaria, it also branched out, adding AIDS prevention to its list of championed causes. Because the stigma of taking an HIV test is so strong, many Africans are reluctant to do so. To overcome this fear and to motivate rural Africans to take HIV tests, Vestergaard Frandsen began to offer a free "CarePack®" to each individual tested. A CarePack® is a small, pack containing a water purifier, a bed net, 60 condoms and health education pamphlets. Thanks to the firm's promotional efforts and the free CarePacks, more than 50,000 Africans were tested for HIV at a cost to Vestergaard Frandsen exceeding $3 million.[67] This was done to prove that it is possible to massively scale-up testing and counseling activities and that by integrating different disease interventions you achieve higher cost-effectiveness.

One of the issues Vestergaard-Frandsen faced in its latest five-year review and strategic planning process was the challenging economic climate around the globe. With declining funding available to governments and international agencies to purchase its products and meet the UN's Millennium Development Goals [see below], the company had to modify its business model. "In carrying out our review, we realized that our LifeStraw® product not only provides clean water, but it saves trees in certain areas of the world since the most common way of purifying water is by boiling it on a wood fire. " Sanne Fournier-Wendes continued "our new approach called for us to give away nearly one million LifeStraw® Family water purifiers and sell the carbon credits to pay for our product.

According to the Vestergaard Frandsen website in April and May, 2011, approximately 900,000 LifeStraw Family water filters were distributed "to

---

66 Personal interview. Lausanne Switzerland. June 24,2011

67 "A Company Prospers by Saving Poor People's Lives." The New York Times. February 2, 2009.
http://www.nytimes.com/2009/02/03/health/research/03prof.html?pagewanted=2&_r=1

approximately 90% of all households in the Western Province of Kenya. The distribution program, called "LifeStraw Carbon for Water," provided more than four million residents with quick access to safe drinking water at home. VF's expenses will be reimbursed by carbon financing. This funding model gives companies in developed countries potential revenue, in the form of carbon credits, for reducing greenhouse gas emissions in developing countries. Carbon credits can then be sold to carbon credit buyers that want to reduce their carbon footprint or improve their environmental stewardship. The revenue generated, in large part, will be re-invested into the program to make it sustainable over a 10- year period. Once the initiative is operational, monitoring by an accredited independent auditor will take place every six months to verify use of the filters and emissions reductions. The auditor will verify that the emission reductions are accurate, and carbon credits will be issued after each verification. The program is led and solely funded by Vestergaard Frandsen and is estimated to cost approximately USD$25 million and the program should produce more than two million tons of carbon emission reductions annually. The company will sell the credits from these reductions to recoup its initial investment and sustain the program. Carbon credit financing is set up as a pay-for-performance business model whereby revenue is only obtained if the technology works and the project achieves carbon emission reductions.[68]

Mikkel Vestergaard Frandsen in his 2009 Corporate Social Responsibility Report says: "In the current financial climate, investments from the growing list of companies seeking to make a positive contribution to global public health need to be more deliberate and specific. These contributions benefit not just their bottom lines, but also empower communities in developing nations." Mikkel adds "our business model of 'humanitarian entrepreneurship' has done both."[69]

"We have seen how private-public partnerships have matured over the last decade to a point where today there is neither controversy about, nor conflict

---

[68] http://www.vestergaard-frandsen.com/carbon-for-water/how-it-works.html
[69] By aligning the company's goals with the UN's Millennium Development Goals it addresses the needs of the 84% of the population without access to an improved source of drinking water who live in rural areas and those afflicted by malaria which according to the WHO imposes a growth penalty of 1.3% per year on some African nations by incapacitating the workforce, leading to decreased productivity.

between, doing business and doing good," Mikkel said in his leadership interview with the Roll Back Malaria Partnership. "At Vestergaard, we have turned corporate social responsibility into our core business by dedicating our entire innovative platform to developing lifesaving technologies and concepts for people in the developing world. Our environmental agenda in relation to bed net production includes continuous optimization to reduce waste and increase recycling. This work is assisted by an environmental audit program. We have taken a major step in packing all nets in biodegradable bags, which will help reduce the environmental impact in the countries that receive our nets."[70]

Vestergaard Frandsen is known worldwide today for its products PermaNet®, ZeroFly® and LifeStraw®. Its products promote public health, reducing child mortality, and prevent the transmission of malaria and other diseases. In 2008, Mikkel Vestergaard Frandsen received the Saatchi & Saatchi Award for World Changing Ideas for LifeStraw®. Not surprisingly, he committed the prize money to providing his life-saving device to people in developing nations, where about 6,000 each day die from a lack of safe water.[71] Mikkel and the company have won subsequent awards from The Economist, The Financial Times, The World Economic Forum and other leading publications and organizations.

Humanitarian Entrepreneurship

The firm has come a long way, evolving from its humble beginnings as a regional clothing manufacturer into a global humanitarian leader with a staff of 200, headquarters in Lausanne, Switzerland, and branch offices in Ghana, India, Indonesia, Kenya, Nigeria, South Africa, the UAE and the USA. Vestergaard Frandsen also operates laboratories in Ghana and Vietnam, and production facilities in Belgium, China, India, Korea, Thailand and Vietnam.[72]

---

[70] www.rollbackmalaria.org/globaladvocacy/leadershipinterviews6.html

[71] In 2009 received the Social and Economic Innovation Award from The Economist and in 2010 the Financial Times Social Innovation Award for Most innovative Small For-Profit Company. The LifeStraw was named one of "10 Things That Will Change the Way We Live" by Forbes in 2006.

[72] Vestergaard Frandsen is still a family-owned business and does not disclose financial data, but the

"We know we're helping when we see thousands of people cueing up outside a clinic to get what we offer," says Mikkel. "We're focusing our business skills on developing a culture of trade for lifesaving products; we're focusing our investments on building factories and scaling up access to lifesaving products. This might not be capitalism in its purist form but it's business, it's doing good and it's fun." [73]

The company has been consistently profitable, [though as it is privately owned and not publicly traded, sales and profitability data is not published]. According to Sanne Fournier-Wendes "like any other private company we generate profits by the sale of our products to our customers, which in our case are mostly public agencies. The difference between us and our competitors is that we reinvest our profits in a range of social products related to our core mission. And this model has allowed us to grow dramatically."[74]

Vestergaard Frandsen's mission is to improve the health of the poor. Together its efforts over the years and its focus on "humanitarian entrepreneurship," which the firm defines as the ability to do business and do good at the same time, has earned Vestergaard Frandsen a solid place as a Good Company. With everything from research to design to the material and distribution, Vestergaard Frandsen keeps the end-users needs paramount. Kevin Starace, malaria advisor for the United Nations said "Vestergaard is just different from other companies we work with. They think of the end-user as a consumer rather than a patient or a victim."[75]

---

company has sold over 165 million nets. Forbes reported that Vestergaard Frandsen earned $5 million pretax on sales of $40 million in 2005.

[73] http://www.youtube.com/watch?v=1bjBxo0mkJw

[74] Personal interview. Lausanne Switzerland. June 24,2011

[75] "A Company Prospers by Saving Poor People's Lives" The New York Times. Feb 2, 2009.

Vestergaard Frandsen—Achieving the UN Millennium Development Goals

Vestergaard Frandsen believes strongly in humanitarian responsibility. The company's commitment to the UN's Millennium Development Goals drives its business objectives and provides the impetus for a continued focus on innovation.

Goal 1: Eradicate extreme poverty and hunger

84% of the population without access to an improved source of drinking water lives in rural areas. Malaria imposes a growth penalty of 1.3% per year on some African nations by incapacitating the workforce, leading to decreased productivity.

Vestergaard Frandsen's Contribution

PermaNet® long-lasting insecticidal nets and curtains and LifeStraw® safe water interventions minimize the risk of vector-borne and waterborne disease respectively, promoting economic gain by reducing healthcare expenses and increased productivity.

Goal 2: Achieve universal primary education

443 million school days are lost each year due to water-related illness. African children have between 1.6 and 5.4 episodes of malarial fever each year, preventing them from regularly attending school.

Vestergaard Frandsen's Contribution

The consumption of safe drinking water through LifeStraw® prevents children from acquiring diarrhea and other waterborne diseases. Sleeping under a PermaNet® bed net every night helps ensure that children wake up healthy each morning to continue their education.

Goal 3: Promote gender equality and empower women

The average distance that women in Africa and Asia walk to collect water is 6 km. The task of obtaining and carrying water over long distances robs women and young girls of dignity, energy, and time.

Vestergaard Frandsen's Contribution

LifeStraw® and LifeStraw® Family empower women and girls by facilitating access to safe drinking water. LifeStraw® Family works on highly turbid water, which allows women to convert 'dirty' water collected from any nearby source into a drinkable one.

Goal 4: Reduce child mortality

Every 30 seconds a child dies from malaria. It is estimated that 5.5 lives could be saved for every 1,000 children that are protected by insecticide-treated nets. Diarrheal diseases claim more than 6,000 lives per day-most of them children under five. The risk of dying from diarrhea is 11 times greater for infants who are HIV-infected.

Vestergaard Frandsen's Contribution

Randomized trials of bed nets have shown a 50% reduction in malaria and a 17% reduction in all cause mortality among children. Point-of-use water filters have been shown to reduce incidence of diarrhea by 64%. LifeStraw® and LifeStraw® Family are both point-of-use water filters.

Goal 5: Improve maternal health

Some 50 million pregnant women are exposed to malaria each year, with malaria in pregnancy contributing to nearly 20% of low birth weight babies in endemic areas. In Africa, up to 200,000 newborn deaths occur as a result of malaria in pregnancy.

Vestergaard Frandsen's Contribution

Studies have shown that when compared to a situation in which no nets were used, ITNs such as PermaNet® reduce the rate of miscarriage/ stillbirth by 33%.

CHAPTER 5

THE SEMCO GROUP

A company full of crazy people? A group of nutters? If you think that Semco is something along these lines, you're not entirely wrong. However, it is not by chance that unconventional ideas are created at this company. They are created and managed within an open management model, different from conventional models, and this is exactly what we want.[76]

RICARDO SEMLER

Semco is an unusual company. Since the 1980s, the company has been on a path to transform itself into a humane, trusting, and productive business that puts employees first. That is not just lip service: Semco treats employees—from the highest ranking executive to the lowest-level clerk—equally. It gives employees the ability to work with substantial freedom, and the opportunity to take ownership of their slice of the company. Its 30-year-old experiment has proved successful: between 1980 and 2010, the company grew from about $1 million in annual sales to annual sales surpassing $300 million.

Semco is fully aware that its model is unusual and it says so on its website.

But Semco, which built its reputation as a manufacturer of mixing machines and marine pumps, was not always this way. Founded in 1953 by Antonio Curt Semler, an Austrian immigrant to Brazil, the firm was a moribund, old-line company with a traditional military-style, top-down hierarchy until the 1980s when Semler resigned as CEO and turned ownership over to his son, Ricardo, then 21, a self-styled iconoclast. Ricardo had always resisted his

---

[76] http://semco.locaweb.com.br/en/content.asp?content=3

father's traditional top- down style of management and sought to diversify away from the struggling shipbuilding industry.

An Employee Centered Business Model

On his first day as CEO, Ricardo Semler fired 60 percent of all top managers and set out to reorganize and modernize the company. During the next few years, the company acquired manufacturing companies like Hobart Brazil and expanded Semco's product lines to include mixers for the chemical, pharmaceutical, food, and mining industries, as well as industrial refrigeration equipment, air-conditioning systems, and food processors. The young Semler also established new financial controls and aggressive marketing, which propelled the company forward.

A series of fainting spells when he was just 25 forced Semler to rethink the business model that had created high levels of stress throughout the company. He realized that, although he had made significant changes, his father's top-down management style and close, distrustful supervision still remained; it alienated employees and caused stress and inefficiencies. Although the firm appeared highly organized and well disciplined, employees were not happy with their jobs. Indeed, few employees felt connected to the value they produced.

These realizations led Semler to seek to create a better work-life balance for himself and his employees. "I couldn't help thinking that Semco could be run differently, without counting everything, without regulating everyone, without keeping track of whether people were late, without all those numbers and all those rules," he thought to himself. "What if we could run the business in a simpler way, a more natural way? A natural business, that's what I wanted."[77]

Semler felt that centralization, which fosters alienation 'like stagnant ponds breed algae,' was the source of the company's problems. "In massive corporations, an employee will know few of his colleagues," he said. "Everyone

---

[77] Ricardo Semler, (1993) Maverick. Warner Books p. 66

is part of a gigantic, impersonal machine, and it's impossible to feel motivated when you feel you are just another cog."[78]

Employees Set their Wages

Casting about, Semler first decided to change the organization and improve communications. "I went ahead and asked our employees at each of our business units to form committees comprised of representatives from every part of the operation but management," he explained. "Every group would have a delegate on these committees, which would meet regularly with top management"[79] The committees set about improving working conditions by painting offices and ordering new furniture.

Gradually, the committees gained confidence. They began setting production goals and suggesting changes in product lines and personnel.

Then, in 1986, due in part to quixotic government leadership, Brazil entered a period of economic instability that hit Semco where it hurt: sales dropped by 40 percent over three years. The committees stepped up; with management's approval, they took responsibility, sharing authority to run the plant, to strategies and policies, and to decide on investments. Committees with union representation went farther, auditing the books and questioning all aspects of management.

"When plants faced hard times, their factory committees would take the initiative and lower wages or increase hours, saving money and protecting jobs," explained Semler. "When layoffs were unavoidable, the committees got involved in the sensitive and unfortunate task of deciding who would go. Together we tried to be socially just, taking into consideration such factors as a worker's history with the company, loyalty, ability to find a new job, and family commitments."[80]

Then Semco's management took an unheard of step: it allowed employees to set their own salaries. "We ask our employees, 'Tell us how much you intend to work. Tell us how much you need in exchange and how much you will produce,'" Semler said.

---

[78] Semler (1993) p. 110
[79] Semler (1993) p. 75
[80] Semler (1993) p. 79

How this works is that employees survey wages at competitors and review this in relation to the company's profits. They use this information to set a desired wage, but if an employee seeks a salary that is out of line with their contribution to production, then they may not be retained. Semler states that peer pressure to perform is a key element in making the system work. [81]

Employees are also empowered to hire new employees and managers. How does that work? "We trust the process," Semler told BizEd magazine in 2004. "We're never sure that we hired right, but then, no organization is. We just reduce the risk. So we bring in many Semco people to interview every candidate—dozens, sometimes—and the candidate comes back many, many times before hiring occurs. Our turnover rate of one percent bears [our success] out."[82]

Semler further departed from the traditional model by adding a unique profit sharing system, opening the company's books, educating employees, and relying on them for innovation.

Speaking to the former, Semler explains that "it has been rooted in the corporate consciousness that profits belong to those who invest the capital. Of course this is the rule even at companies at which the founder originally invested very little and which grew largely because of the energy and talents of the employees."[83] After some negotiation, employees and management together designed the Semco Profit-Sharing Program (SemcoPar), in which one-fourth of corporate profits are divided equally among employees.

To assist in the financial education of employees, Semco, together with the union, developed a cartoon guide to reading and understanding the company's financial information. In yet another non-traditional move designed to release the creative energy of employees, Semco created the Nucleus of Technological Innovation (NTI), a small group of engineers released from day-to-day responsibilities and given the freedom to invent new products, devise new strategies, uncover cost reductions, or develop new lines of business.

---

[81] AME Info.
[82] Shinn Sharon (2004)"The Maverick CEO". BizEd Magazine.
[83] Semler (10993) p 138

Community Benefits

The firm also seeks to influence and create change outside its corporate walls. In the 1990s, Semler created the Ralston-Semler Foundation to be a catalyst for a range of educational, cultural, environmental, and strategic projects, including:

The Lumiar Institute, a center for studies that holds debates, performs research, and reflects on democratic education during childhood and adolescence to implement democratic education at several schools. The Institute was among 12 schools worldwide to receive recognition and support from the Gates Foundation.

The DNA Brazil Institute, a think tank promoting strategic studies for Brazil.

Habitat dos Mellos (Mellos' Habitat), an environmental project that seeks to reconstitute the native forest and help economic growth in the Mellos region while respecting the local culture.

Semco has also developed environmental consultancies, facilities management firms, real estate consultancies, and inventory and mobile maintenance services companies. In 2006, the company formed BRENCO (Brazilian Renewable Energy Company) to work in biofuel development.

Today, Semco is considered the market leader in the industrial equipment arena and in solutions for postal and document management. Almost every Semco employee sets his or her own schedule. When employees are tired or if they need a mental break, they visit the outdoor room and rest or think in a hammock. At Semco, it is clear that employees matter.

Lessons for Others

So what are the lessons for other companies? Can other companies learn from Semco and could they implement these practices? Ricardo Semler, now Chairman of the Semco Group of companies, speaks frequently around the world. During one such occasion, he told BizEd Magazine that Semco offers lessons for everyone. "There are many standalone concepts," he explained. "One is the idea of a 360-degree evaluation, which we instituted in 1979, or of candidates for leadership jobs being interviewed by their future subordinates, or even the idea of people working at home—which we've been practicing since 1981. Many companies would encounter difficulties convincing bosses to give up control, which is a basic tenet at Semco. But there are also thousands of company owners who could implement freedoms and don't. Finally," says Semler, "there is a long series of little things that each person can do within his or her sphere of influence. These things can change lifestyles and create gratification. It doesn't require all or nothing. The main lesson is that freedom is a prime driver for performance."[84]

SEMCO GROUP PRINCIPLES AND VALUES

1 – To be a dependable and reliable company;

2 – Value honesty and transparency over and above all temporary interests;

3 – Seek a balance between short-term and long-term profit;

4 – Offer products and services at fair prices which are recognized by customers as the best on the market;

5 – Provide the customer with differentiated services, placing our responsibility before profits;

6 – Encourage creativity, giving support to the bold;

7 – Encourage everyone's participation and question decisions that are imposed from the top down;

8 – Maintain an informal and pleasant environment, with a professional attitude and free of preconceptions;

9 – Maintain safe working conditions and control industrial processes to protect our personnel and the environment;

10 – Have the humility to recognize our errors and understanding that we can always improve.

---

[84] Sharon Shinn.(2004) "The Maverick CEO". BizEd

Financial Results

According to an article in Strategy and Business in 2006, "An investment of $100,000 made in Semco 20 years ago would be worth $5.4 million today — a rare record of profitability that by all accounts stems directly from the participative management approach that Mr. Semler champions."[85] Clearly Semco's distinctive principles and values, outlined in the box SEMCO Company Principles and Values, and its belief in the humane, equal treatment of employees, is what makes the firm a Good Company.

---

[85] Strategy and Business. Issue 41 2006.

CHAPTER 6

TRIODOS BANK

The financial crisis of 2008 started as a rumble on Wall Street banks and then became a tsunami that crashed on banks and financial markets affecting communities, municipalities and workers around the world. The main cause of this financial meltdown was a wave of mortgage-backed artificial securities like collateralized debt obligations (CDOs) and credit default swaps (CDSs). Wall Street investment banks fueled a speculative boom which became a financial bubble. When the bubble burst, the fallout left the world's economies reeling. Any trust in a financial system which was seen as devoid of any ethics evaporated as bank failures sky-rocked. Relatively few large banks were unscathed.[86] Triodos Bank, one of the world leaders in ethical banking was untouched by Wall Street's mess. This chapter tells us why.

Founded in 1980 and based in the Netherlands and with branches in Belgium, Germany the UK and Spain, its name, Triodos comes from the Greek "tri-hodos" signifying the bank's consideration of three values: culture, people and the environment in all investment decisions. Emphasizing its leadership in the height of the world financial crisis, CEO Peter Blom stated

---

[86] For a cogent, clear and compelling explanation of how Wall Street greed created unprecedented weapons of mass financial destruction which wrecked the economy see Les Leopold, The Looting of America, Chelsea Green 2009.

"We want to help build a more sustainable financial system and think that our banking model will inspire profound changes in the mainstream banking industry." Blom got his start as an economics student who needed money to renovate a natural foods restaurant in Amsterdam in 1977. Where did he get the loan?-from the Triodos Foundation, a precursor of Triodos Bank. Blom later went on to work for the bank rising to become its CEO.

What is it that makes Triodos Bank different? The company's mission is "to make money work for positive social, environmental and cultural change." The company website indicates "We only lend our customers' money to people and organizations working to make the world a better place, actively seeking out and promoting sustainable, entrepreneurial businesses driven by values and ideas - rather than just refusing to back businesses that do harm."[87]

Triodos' Business Model

Triodos clients include over 9,500 companies, organic farms, fair trade initiatives, social enterprises and non-profits judged to be social or environmental leaders. The bank's funds come from over 260,000 depositors. A study of the bank's financial performance showed that between 1999 and 2003 Triodos Bank achieved a growth of 21 percent compared with only 8 percent in its peer group of financial institutions.[88] Triodos has earned a profit every year since its inception. During 2010, Triodos Bank's balance sheet total increased by more than 11% to EUR 3.3 billion. Triodos Bank's operating profit rose by 27% compared to the same period in 2009.

Triodos Bank's success can be directly attributed to its simple business model: The company only lends money to entrepreneurs we know well and for causes that its depositors support. The bank did not invest in complex financial instruments which proved disastrous for so many other banks. This approach has enabled Triodos Bank not just to remain a bulwark of stability in a time of global financial crisis, but to continue growing.

A turning point in the bank's history was the Chernobyl disaster in 1986. Inspired by the impact and extent of the disaster, the company decided to

---

[87] www.triodos.com
[88] David Porteus. Private Development Banking: Managing the Tensions. Citied in Marco Vissher. Banking on Change; Ode. Jan/Feb 2006 pp. 43-49.

develop its own environmental initiatives, to invest in wind parks and alternatives to dangerous nuclear energy. As a result, sustainable energy received a strong boost and the Netherlands became an international leader in the field.

Triodos website states that "everyone should have equal rights and freedom to pursue their personal development and economic interests. And that they should be able to do so while taking responsibility for the consequences their actions have on society and the planet." Consequently they follow a triple bottom line policy of seeking to optimize its treatment of its people, its treatment of the planet while earning a profit.

"Our approach is based on the fundamental belief that economic activity can and should have a positive impact on society, the environment and culture. We value people, planet and profit - and take all three into account in everything we do. We call this sustainable banking. And it explains why we invest only in, or lend only to, organizations that contribute to a more sustainable society."[89]

Wouldn't it be good to know exactly what your bank does with your money—who it is lending to, and what they are doing with it? Triodos customers can target a cause that would receive a portion of the interest earned from their savings account. And wealthier borrowers pay higher rates for loans, in contrast with typical banking practice. The bank also substitutes 'personal security' whereby a group of people could act as guarantors for a risky new venture.

The global financial crisis has led to calls for banks to be more transparent, though it is hard to imagine being able to log on to the website of Citibank, Chase or Barclay's Bank and find out the names and addresses of every business and organization they have lent to. But that's just what Triodos does. It's customers – and anyone else for that matter, can learn more about the hundreds of projects they are funding, looking by keyword such as organic, wind or fair trade to see just to which companies their money goes.

Triodos only finances those that create social, environmental or cultural "added value". These range from organic farms, renewable energy ventures

---

[89] www.triodos.com

and recycling businesses, to projects for the homeless and community cinemas.[90] Triodos carefully screens companies before investing in them and excludes from investment any company that produces or distributes nuclear energy, or components to generate nuclear energy. Nor can any company earn any revenue from selling environmentally hazardous chemicals, pornography, tobacco or weapons.

The bank's lending criteria give specific guidelines indicating the kind of investments they seek to support. Triodos supports producers of sustainable products or services , which they define as services that contribute to create a clean planet, protect the climate or to keep people healthy.

The bank's investment policy states: "Through our stock market investments we want to encourage companies to make a positive contribution to a clean earth and the development of sustainable solutions for environmental pollution. This is an urgent issue, because our natural environment is under increasing pressure. Companies that are active in this field are usually involved in new developments with respect to environmental technology aimed at combating pollution and cleaning up the earth. Companies that specialize in recording environmental pollution and energy consumption are also categorized within this theme".[91]

Triodos values transparency and states "We strongly believe depositors should know how their money is used." Clients and the public can view the bank's lending practices on their website under a heading "Know Where Your Money Goes". Triodos supports companies like AES Solar which develops, finances, constructs, owns and operates utility-scale solar photovoltaic power plants globally, Zaytoun, a fair trade organization established to support farming communities in Palestine, and Nautia Housing Co-operative, a housing co-operative with all members involved in social and environmental projects, particularly organic food production and distribution.

---

[90] Rupert Jones (2009) Triodos Bank Where Transparency is the Best Policy. Oct 3, 2009 retrieved from www.guardian.co.uk/money/2009/oct/03/
[91] Triodos Bank Investment Criteria January 2009 p. 1.

An Environmental Leader

According to the bank's website: "Too often, sustainability is seen as one of many competing priorities, rather than an integral part of successful growth. Although an increasing number of people agree – in principle – with the need for fundamental change, decision makers have been slow to do anything about it. Triodos Bank provides a clear example of how integrated sustainability can be the key to financial growth."

The bank launched some of the first green and culture funds and is a global leader in micro- finance. Triodos refuses to invest in companies that don't contribute to a better world and carefully scrutinizes borrowers to ensure that they meet the bank's strict social and environmental criteria. For example, in a recent exchange with the Board of Directors of Phillips, the electronics conglomerate illustrates the work of Triodos research department.

Triodos advocates directly linking sustainability performance to managerial compensation and " sought clarification on the criteria that the company uses to define its so-called Green Products and to push for more environmental targets [and] asked that the company use sustainability indicators to assess Management's performance and to determine its financial compensation."[92]

In a meeting with Barclay's Bank, Triodos encouraged the company to raise its ethical standards. "The main topic of the meeting was the involvement in controversial weapons, i.e. anti-personnel mines and cluster bombs. There is a growing global movement away from these weapons, but Barclays is not prepared to end business relationships with companies that happen to be involved in controversial weapons. However, the company agreed to strengthen its screening and assessment process for these companies and refer to the Oslo Treaty (cluster munitions) and the Ottawa Treaty (land mines) in its internal policy and guidance."[93]

In 2009, the bank was awarded the Financial Times Sustainable Bank of the Year for its leadership and innovation in integrating sustainability into all of its activities. In making the award the judges indicated that Triodos Bank "had raised an important question as to whether the financial crisis prompted

---

[92] www.triodos.com/com/triodos_research
[93] www.triodos.com/com/triodos_research

a review of the business model of the industry and what the new model should be like. The exceptional application of Triodos showed the emergence of a particular type of financial institution which is combining sustainability considerations not only within the organization but also financing only sustainable companies, thereby accelerating the move towards a more sustainable economy. The potential of the model has been shown by an exceptional financial performance."[94]

The bank rates well with respect to all of the good company criteria: employees are treated with respect, Triodos incorporates environmental sustainability in every aspect of its business operations, through its foundation and its lending policies the bank directly supports the community, and Triodos has been consistently profitable since its foundation.

TRIODOS BANK'S KEYS TO SUCCESS

1. A sustainable business model
We have a simple business model. We only lend money entrusted to us by savers and investors, to entrepreneurs we know well. Because we work in the real economy we don't invest in complex financial instruments that promise high profits but also bring greater risk. It may sound old-fashioned, but it's an approach that has enabled Triodos Bank not just to remain solid and stable in a time of global financial crisis, but also to continue growing rapidly.

2. Positively 100% sustainable
We only lend our customers' money to people and organizations working to make the world a better place, actively seeking out and promoting sustainable, entrepreneurial businesses driven by values and ideas—rather than just refusing to back businesses that do harm.

3. Total transparency
We believe that sustainable banking depends on trust, so we publish details of every single organization we lend to which means our savers and investors can see exactly how we're using their money.

---

[94] "Sustainable Bank of the Year Clinched by Triodos bank" www.blog.Littlecowarrior.co.uk/tag/triodos-bank.

CHAPTER 7

TOMS SHOES

"With every pair purchased, TOMS will give a pair of new shoes to a child in need. One for One."

When he decided to start a global shoe company, Blake Mycoskie was a 29-year old entrepreneur with zero fashion industry experience. His inspiration was not easy profits or a love for shoes, but rather a desire to provide shoes to children around the world who suffer from debilitating illnesses and injuries as a result of not having them.

A Unique Model for Serving the Community

The company Mycoskie founded is TOMS Shoes. TOMS designs and sells a line of unique shoes made of light-weight fabrics, inspired by the traditional rope soled shoe of Argentina, "the alpargata." Blake Mycoskie's vision for the company originated on a vacation he took to Argentina. Struck by the poverty and health issues in Argentina and the desire to "do more", Mycoskie set out to introduce the alpargata to the U.S. market in order to "make life more comfortable for those without shoes." To fulfill this purpose, Mycoskie made a promise: for every pair of TOMS Shoes purchased, one pair of TOMS Shoes would be donated to a child in need. The business plan is simple: 'one for one.' To date, TOMS has given over 140,000 children their first pair of shoes.[95]

In the United States and throughout Europe, children from even the poorest families grow up being able to afford to wear shoes; however, poor children in many developing countries grow up walking barefoot. And walking is often a primary mode of transportation for these children. They may walk miles for food, water, and shelter or to go to school. Whether they are playing, doing chores, or just conducting day-to-day activities, working or walking barefoot creates major health risks. The conditions they live through are often inconceivable to most of us in the United States. [96]

Shoes are more than just a comfort or modern convenience; wearing shoes prevents feet from injuries as a result of walking on unsafe roads and contaminated soil. Infected wounds can be very painful and dangerous, and may result in amputation. A leading cause of disease in developing countries is soil-transmitted parasites which penetrate the skin through open sores.

One such disease is podoconiosis (commonly referred to as 'Podo'). Podo is caused by simply walking or working barefoot in silica-heavy, volcanic soil, a very common practice in rural farming regions of developing countries. This disfiguring disease is caused by walking barefoot on heavily silica-based soil of volcanic origin. The silica gets into the lymphatic system and blocks the ducts, basically destroying the lymphatic system and causing swelling and disfigurement. In Ethiopia alone, 300,000 people are affected, including one in every 13 Ethiopian children. The disabling effects of Podoconiosis cause great hardship to patients. It adversely affects their economic and social standing, in the community, and it also affects their psychological well-being.

This creates a large public health problem in at least ten countries in tropical Africa, Central America and northern India.

Most importantly, Podo is 100% preventable by wearing shoes.

Often, schools in even the poorest countries require shoes for children in attendance. If children do not have shoes, they cannot attend school. Not

---

[95] TOMS Shoes.com "Our Movement"http://www.tomsshoes.com/content.asp?tid=271
[96] TOMS Shoes.com "Our Movement"

receiving an education greatly limits their ability or opportunity to realize their potential.

There are many organizations who seek to provide shoes (new or used) to children in underdeveloped countries, but with ever growing populations the demand continues to outpace the supply that these non-profits can offer. The manufacture or collection, transport, and distribution of shoes to those who need them offers the same challenges (including financial) that any global company would face in the distribution of its goods and services. Unfortunately, the consequences of failing to overcome these challenges can be dire for children living in underdeveloped countries without shoes.

TOMS Shoes was started by Mycoskie in 2006 with $300,000 of his own savings. He was already a successful entrepreneur who had created and sold four businesses. In 2002, Mycoskie and his sister participated in The Amazing Race, a reality television game show in which teams race around the world in competition with other teams. Mycoskie and his sister lost the $1 million prize by four minutes, but both gained a love for international travel. After the show, Mycoskie spent time traveling back to many of the countries he had visited during taping of the show.[97]

In January 2006, Mycoskie went back to Argentina to vacation, explore the culture, and learn to play polo. While there, he noticed that many of the villages lived with the bare minimum of modern conveniences that many people in the United States have grown up with. He also met American aid workers who were collecting donated shoes to take to a village to give to children whose families could not afford shoes. Mycoskie volunteered his time to go along to the villages for the experience. He was immediately struck with the feeling that he wanted to give these children shoes, but not just the one time. He felt that giving them shoes once would only make himself feel good but not solve the issues of needing shoes when a pair wore out or from growing out of them. He was struck by the horrifying disease of podoconiosis that plagued healthy children whose families could not afford shoes. Mycoskie's desire to help these children combined with his entrepreneurial drive sparked his idea for TOMS Shoes.

---

[97] TOMS Shoes: A History, 2009 January 23, 2009). Online company sponsored video retrieved from http://www.youtube.com/watch?v=PTQsQUu1Ho8.

A Social Business Model

Additionally, Mycoskie noticed that the traditional shoe of Argentina, the alpargata, was worn by everyone from businesspeople to athletes to farmers. The shoe was just a simple rope soled canvas slipper which sold for about $4 USD. Mycoskie was intrigued by the shoe design and was convinced that he could improve the concept and sell it in the United States.[98]

Mycoskie's original plan was to call his business the "shoes for tomorrow project," meaning, "buy a pair today, give away a pair tomorrow." Later, he decided to call the firm TOMS Shoes. Often the question arises, "Who is Tom?" TOMS stands for tomorrow, however, Mycoskie explains, "We are all Tom because we can all make a better tomorrow." [99]

Mycoskie's first step in getting his shoe business off the ground was convincing Argentine shoe makers to upgrade the quality of the traditional alpargata while keeping production costs low. He was met with a great deal of resistance due to the fact that the redesigned shoe would be much more expensive to produce, but was successful in convincing one shoemaker to work with him.

The redesigned shoe added a rubber sole, arch support, leather insoles and high quality fabrics. Mycoskie ordered an initial 250 prototype pairs of shoes, based on the number of children in the village he originally visited, and planned to sell them in Los Angeles, at $40 per pair. With the profit earned, he would return to Argentina to give the same number of shoes to the children in the village. Mycoskie estimated that it would take him six months to sell the shoes and he planned to go back to Argentina during the holiday season. Mycoskie headed back to Los Angeles with pictures of his shoes and pictures of the kids in Argentina. He emailed the pictures to 24 top LA boutiques hoping they would be interested in his product. He received only one email back from a shoe buyer for the American Rag boutique. The buyer

---

[98] Katie Bryan and Tania Linsey. TOMS Shoes/Frontera Foods, *(Television episode) The Entrepreneurs.* New Jersey: CNBC.April 2, 2009 *Also see "PhiLAnthropist Interview: TOMS Shoes Founder Blake Mycoskie Plans to Give Away 300,000 Pairs in 2009." LAist online magazine.* *http://laist.com/2009/04/15/what_happens_when_you_travel.php*

[99] TOMS Shoes: A History, 2009

was very interested in Mycoskie's cause, and additionally, thought the shoes were "cool" and had a good price point. She ordered 150 pairs to sell in the LA boutique.[100]

Within four months, Mycoskie's inventory was down to sixty pairs and a big breakthrough that would essentially change his life and the future of TOMS occurred when a writer for the LA Times, Booth Moore, had heard about his mission. On May 20, 2006, an extensive article was published on the cover of the Calendar section of the newspaper. By 2 P.M., he had sold 2,200 pairs of TOMS via the company's website. Up to this time, Mycoskie had been working alone out of his loft apartment.

In order to meet the high demand, he solicited assistance through Craigslist and by Tuesday he hired three interns. The interns had the task of emailing every customer to let them know that the shoes would not be delivered in two days as promised on the website, rather, the delivery date would be closer to two months. Mycoskie traveled back to Argentina to set up production to meet the unexpected high sales. Mycoskie was able to find one fabric maker who believed in his mission and production was started. [101]

Many people did not believe that Mycoskie's "one for one" business model would turn a profit; however, profit was not Mycoskie's goal. He simply wanted to be able to sustain the business and give shoes to children in need. Mycoskie loved the drive and the challenge it took to start this business and carry out his mission. Within a month, he was able to fulfill the order of 2,200 pairs of shoes. Then the media buzz and publicity surrounding TOMS grew extensively and shoe sales skyrocketed. Within its first five months, the company sold over 10,000 pairs of shoes generating $400,000 in sales. In October 2006, Mycoskie returned to Argentina with friends, family and interns to donate 10,000 pairs of shoes to the children who had inspired him. These visits are now called "TOMS Shoe Drops" where the shoes are hand placed with every child. The success of the first TOMS Shoe Drop proved to Mycoskie that his one-for-one business model could work.

One of the ways TOMS has sought to diversify and be sustainable is through its line of eco- friendly vegan shoes sold exclusively at Whole Foods Markets.

---

[100] Bryan, 2009.
[101] Bryan, 2009.

These shoes are made of hemp and eco-poly (a polyester that is made from recycled water bottles), and the soles are made of recycled rubber. Amazingly, this is the fastest growing accessory ever to sell in Whole Foods (Bryan 2009).

TOMS uses Intertek to monitor their overseas production facilities and has been recognized by many outside entities. Intertek performs a third party audit of Tom's Shoes labor regulations since they manufacture shoes in China, Argentina, and Ethiopia. They validate products, processes, and operations -- providing assurance of regulatory compliance, product quality, monitoring supply chain regulations, workplace safety, and social accountability. In addition TOMS production teams visit the factories at least once a year to audit labor conditions, wage and labor standards, and to make sure they maintain the expected work standards (TOMS, 2011).

The company says its best advertisement is word of mouth and everybody who wears a pair of TOMS becomes an unofficial spokesperson for the company. TOMS goes to great lengths to engage their customers in its movement. Mycoskie founded a not-for-profit sister company called Friends of TOMS whose mission is to support TOMS by creating and coordinating avenues for individuals to volunteer and experience the one-for-one movement in action. This may be by participating in a TOMS Shoe Drop, which are open to anyone who wants to volunteer, or by providing financial or medical support for the cause. TOMS believes that people want to do good, and Friends of TOMS facilitates opportunities to put good intentions into action.

In an interview with Business Week Magazine in 2009, Mycoskie said "TOMS is different from the other companies I have started: It combines my love of entrepreneurship and my desire to help others. When I was a student at Southern Methodist University in 1998, I met entrepreneur Bob Dedman, the man behind ClubCorp. He was a self-made billionaire who was also incredibly philanthropic. He gave away $200 million. At the time, I had just started my laundry business and I asked him for a piece of business advice. He told me: 'The more you give, the more you live.' I have always kept Bob's advice in the back of my mind." [102]

---

[102] Stacy Perman, (January 23, 2009) "Making a Do-gooder's Business Model Work." *Business Week Online Magazine.* Retrieved from

Less than three years after it was created, TOMS was in an 8,000 square foot warehouse in Santa Monica with forty-five full time staff and twenty-two interns and a network of volunteers all over the world. TOMS may not reach the financial success of Nike, who makes $18 Billion a year, but Mycoskie has found success by simply being able to pay his staff, make a small profit, build a brand, and do what he set out to do in the beginning: provide shoes to children in need of them. TOMS is now sold in Nordstrom's department stores and hundreds of independent shoe retailers across the country. Consumers can find TOMS in eight countries.

"If I would've taken half a million dollars and just bought shoes to give to the kids, I would've been able to give the shoes once. It never would've been as far-reaching and sustainable as TOMS Shoes is now." Mycoskie has said that he knows this company will never be huge, but he wants it to be strong and for it to be able to be successful enough to keep giving back.

TOMS pays attention to the product, the people they are affecting, and the financial health of the company. In order to maintain or improve profitability, TOMS has been expanding into clothing and eyewear and new styles of shoes are constantly being created. The company controls costs using social media, Facebook, blogs, Twitter, televised media, viral videos, and YouTube, to gain awareness in the market place, all without spending money on advertising.

The employees are proud to be a part of this company so it is supported and sustained that way. The business model is self-sustaining, rather than a one-time charity and it keeps giving. Using this "One to One" business model, as of September 2010, TOMS Shoes had donated over one million pairs of shoes throughout Argentina, Ethiopia, South Africa and the U.S.

In 2007, TOMS was honored with the prestigious People's Design Award from the Cooper-Hewitt National Design Museum, Smithsonian Institution. Two years later, Blake and TOMS received the 2009 ACE award by Secretary of State Hillary Clinton, which recognizes companies' commitment to corporate social responsibility, innovation, exemplary practices, and democratic values worldwide (TOMS, 2011).

---

http://www.businessweek.com/smallbiz/content/jan2009/sb20090123_264702.htm

Lisebeth den Toom is senior editor of Springwise, an Amsterdam-based blog and newsletter that tracks new business ideas, "Without the connection to a larger cause," she says, "I doubt the TOMS brand would have grown as quickly or had as much staying power."

"But the most important reason may be something deeper. Perhaps the profit motive, while still glorious and necessary, is no longer sufficient for 21st century ventures. Around the world, some of the top-performing businesses are marrying the profit motive with the "purpose motive"—the sense that commercial enterprises should stand for something and contribute to the world." [103]

Emily Bawan, MBA, Michael Gossman, MBA and Ramona Indrebo, EMBA assisted with the research.

---

[103] Daniel Pink. TOMS Shoes' giveaways helps it stamp towards profit. The Telegraph. Oct 10, 2010 retrieved from www.telegraph.co.uk Oct 8, 2011

CHAPTER 8

BENETECH

"The Most Powerful Force on Earth is the Human Mind. At Benetech, we're combining that power with a deep passion for social improvement. Our goal is simple: to create new technology solutions that serve humanity and empower people to improve their lives. Day by day we're helping to build a better, safer world."[104]

Even as a student at Caltech, Jim Fruchterman wanted to build a low-cost reading machine for the blind. Although millions of people needed such a machine, only a few could afford the high cost; that is, until Fruchterman came along.

Fruchterman, while developing a smart missile for military use, kept thinking that there must be a socially valuable way to use this technology—perhaps to help the blind to read. Later as a chip designer at Hewlett-Packard, Fruchterman designed a chip that could read anything. He proposed to his employer, "How about making a reading machine for the blind?"

"Well, just how big is that market?" his supervisor asked. Jim replied, "I think it's in the range of a million dollars a year." "It's too small," his supervisor said. "We're working to develop products for a $100 million market."[105]

---

[104] www.benetech.org/about
[105] Jim Fruchterman presentation to the Social Venture Network October 2008. La Jolla, California.

Fruchterman left the field of rocket science to start Benetech in the early 1990s. He and his colleague David Ross set a goal to develop and distribute technologies whose humanitarian promise dwarfed their potential profit. "We think of ourselves as a high-tech company, but our customers are people who most high-tech companies won't go after," Fruchterman said.[106] Benetech's first product was a machine that, using optical-recognition software inspired by Fruchterman's work on smart bombs, converted printed books to audio books for the blind. At the time, the best available technology to read printed text was the size of a washing machine with a five-figure price tag—clearly, unaffordable and unrealistic for daily tasks like browsing a newspaper and reading mail. And although the technology for building an affordable and portable reading machine existed, the potential customer base was too small to provide investors with an adequate rate of return.

A Lean Value Business Model

But that didn't stop Benetech, which was founded as a low-profit company using a market approach to ensure the development of technology that "promises to have a high social value despite low potential for generating a typical return on investment." The company's goal at its founding was simple: to create new technology solutions that serve humanity and empower people to improve their lives.[107] Benetech's low-profit-market approach enables the development of technology that promises to have a high social value despite a low return on investment.

Today, working like a high-tech start-up, Benetech's management team identifies needs and opportunities where technology could have a major impact. They ask: Does it fill an important need? What is the social impact? For some ideas, the company serves as a 'corporate home,' testing viability and joining forces with strategic partners and philanthropic investors who

---

[106] Carrie Kirby, "Placing people before profit: Palo Alto's Benetech sets out to help human rights organizations save lives" San Francisco Chronicle Monday, April 14, 2003 page E - 1
[107] www.benetech.org

share their 'zeal to better the world.'[108] The company runs a lean social value model, with 85 percent of every dollar going to support its initiatives.

Since it's founding, Benetech has become a bridge connecting business and technology leaders of California's Silicon Valley with the social needs of humanity. "At Benetech, ...our goal is simple: to create new technology solutions that serve humanity and empower people to improve their lives. Day by day, we're helping build a better, safer world."

Serving the Community

Benetech's first product, the Arkenstone Reading Machine, used the optical character recognition (OCR) technology found in scanners to scan and read text aloud using a personal computer. At a cost of less than $2,000, the Arkenstone Reading Machine quickly found a large and growing customer base—blind individuals and their employers, people with learning disabilities, and government agencies serving the disabled—that generated millions in revenue annually and ultimately led to the sale of the Reading Machine to a distributor of products for people with disabilities. Benetech's inexpensive reading machine, developed "by accepting below-average returns, ultimately ended up creating a new and profitable market while serving the thousands of Americans—veterans in particular—who previously were unable to read printed text on their own." [109]

Benetech's second product was inspired by the question, "How can technologists protect peasants in conflict zones from being murdered?" This is a problem in many parts of the world where non-combatant civilians are massacred by unruly armies. As a company of engineers who like to think about all kinds of solutions, Benetech came up with an answer: the Martus Human Rights Bulletin System. This simple database program helps human rights observers who often work in low-tech field offices to maintain records of police brutality, rapes, and other abuses. Benetech's Human Rights program systematically turns thousands of stories into

---

[108] Among the many funding partners are Adobe Corporation, The Hewlett Foundation, Microsoft Foundation, American Bar Association, Truth and Reconciliation Commission, South Africa; O'Reilly Media, UNDP, World Wildlife Fund and The Nature Conservancy.

[109] www.socialedge.org/blogs/government-engagement/topics/Benetech

analyses that human rights defenders can use to prove whether cases of mass violence are isolated incidents or a systematically executed policy. No other organization that we know of dedicates itself to applying technology and scientific methods exclusively to human rights. Benetech's rigorous data processing and analyses are helping to transform the debate about human rights from politics to science.[110] For example:

"In Sri Lanka, the Consortium of Humanitarian Agencies documents thousands of human rights violations in far-flung areas of the country on a shoestring budget and uses Martus to transmit the information to its headquarters in the nation's biggest city, Colombo. The program also has been used in the United States by Arizona's AZ Coalition Against Domestic Violence when it compiled a report on fatalities and murder-suicides."[111]

Benetech also produces Route 66 Literacy, a web-based program that enables the literate to help teenagers and adults learn to read. Miradi is yet another innovative software program, developed as a joint venture between Benetech and a consortium of global conservation organizations committed to improving the practice of conservation. Miradi is designed to help conservation teams prioritize environmental threats and select appropriate indicators to assess the effectiveness of actions.

Operationally, Benetech is much like a startup in a venture capital environment. Team members first identify needs and opportunities where technology could greatly improve the lives of underserved people. They then determine the viability of an idea, and apply research, analyses, and business planning to make decisions on behalf of society, as well as on behalf of limited partners who provide grants, donations, and access to intellectual property.

Financial Results

Benetech's model, which meets all the criteria of a good company, works. "Our return on investment is not measured in dollars," explained

---

[110] www.benetech.org

[111] Carrie Kirby, "Placing people before profit: Palo Alto's Benetech sets out to help human rights organizations save lives" San Francisco Chronicle Monday, April 14, 2003 page E - 1

Fruchterman, "but in the number of lives we affect. This return on humanity will pay off for generations to come."[112] Employees are involved in every aspect of the company's operation. Its drive to sustain the planet is evident through Benetech's products. The company was founded to meet community needs. And finally, the revenues of Benetech are used to further support community activities.

In 2010 Benetech, a non-profit, received revenues of $9.0 million up from $8.7 million in 2009. Of the total, 87 percent came from project revenues, royalties and consulting fees while 13 percent came from contributions and donated services and products. Some 79 percent of the revenues came from the award of a contract with the US Department of Education for Bookshare, which provides people with disabilities instant access to more than 90,000 books and 150 daily newspapers.[113]

There's an old Rabbinical story that says when the Messiah returns he will ask only one question—to see the soles of your feet, which will show whether you wore them out trying to make the world a better place. Jim Fruchterman is one businessman who has, with certainty, worn out the soles of his feet.

---

[112] www.benetech.org
[113] Beneficent Technology, Inc. Independent Auditors Report and Audited Financial Statements 2009 and 2010. June 9, 2011 At the beginning of the year the company's Benetech had net assets of $2.9 million but expenses exceeded revenues by $1.1 million.

CHAPTER 9

TRADITIONAL MEDICINALS

Make sure that the purpose is greater than yourself. If you follow your purpose and ideals and operate in an ethical way, the financial rewards will follow.

DRAKE SADLER, TRADITIONAL MEDICINALS FOUNDER AND CHAIRMAN OF THE BOARD

In the early 1970s, Drake Sadler and two partners began blending and selling teas in a small herb shop in Sebastopol, California. They were doing well financially, but Sadler had a broader vision when he started the company. "An estimated seventy to ninety percent of medicinal plant species are collected in the wild, mainly by local and indigenous people. These native villages are horribly impoverished and struggle to preserve their culture and communities," says Sadler. He wanted to work with these communities in order to help them change their lives from poverty to prosperity. "With the support of our health conscious consumers," he added, "we saw an opportunity to end poverty, end hunger, rebuild families, restore self-sufficiency and economic stability in these rural and indigenous-communities."[114]

In 1974 Sadler's herb shop became Traditional Medicinals, a leader and an example of a business model based on sustainable environmental and social progression for the twenty-first century. The company manufactures over

---

[114] Presentation to Sonoma State University students. September 14, 2010

50 varieties of tea in a facility that produces 75% of its energy needs via solar power. The company is the eighth largest tea company in the US and the largest medicinal, organic[115], and fair trade[116] herbal tea company in the United States. Its products are distributed nationally through natural foods stores, grocery stores, mass-market retailers, and drug stores.

Additionally, Traditional Medicinals is the only herbal tea company in the US to clinically test their tea formulas. As CEO Blair Kellison says, "Our mission is to provide herbal medicines for family healthcare. Our teas contain pharmacopoeial grade herbs—that's the quality of herb necessary to provide the desired effect."[117] Traditional Medicinals' products can be found in Whole Foods, Kroger, Safeway, Target, CVS and even Walmart, as well as most health food stores and groceries. In 2011 the company sold 16 million boxes, up from 13 million in 2010.[118]

Sustainability at Traditional Medicinals

Sustainability is a core value of the company. According to the mission statement on the company's web site, "Traditional Medicinals is committed to providing affordable traditional herbal medicine for family health and welfare. We embrace sustainability, ingredient purity, social and environmental activism."[119]

One gets the clear sense that these values pervade life at Traditional Medicinals. Even the walls of the company's lunch and meeting room are plastered with informational posters titled 'Certified Organic,' 'Fair Trade,' 'Preserving Wild Collection,' 'Mayan Biosphere,' and 'Solar Power.'

---

[115] SPINS/Nielsen Total US Grocery + HNF combined 52 Weeks Ending 2011-Sep-03 Branded Bag Tea with 95-100% Organic Content

[116] SPINS/Nielsen Total US Grocery + HNF combined 52 Weeks Ending 2011-Sep-03 Branded Bag Tea Fair Trade Certified™ by Fair Trade USA

[117] In 1983 the company received the first drug-manufacturing license issued by the FDA to produce OTC (over the counter) plant based drugs using the tea bag as a delivery system. In 1998 the company began manufacturing dietary supplements according to FDA guidelines.

[118] Blair Kellison, presentation April 27, 2011. 37 percent of sales come from three products: Smooth Move, Mother's Milk and Throat Cure.

[119] www.traditionalmedicinals.com

Ariana Spillane, Sales Administrator, says "After a career in real estate and finance I started working with Traditional Medicinals as a temp. That was 12 years ago. I stayed because of our commitment to ethics, to our customers and to the quality of our products. I like the Traditional Medicinals philosophy." [120]

Acting on its environmental commitment, the company uses organic herbs wherever possible, produces 75 percent of its own energy with solar panels while offsetting the remainder with wind energy credits, and utilizes recycled_paper in packaging. As Blair Kellison says, "We were sustainable before it was in vogue. Sustainability is in the DNA of our company and it should be a core value of every company."[121]

For every pound of consumer waste there are an estimated eight pounds of consumer waste in the supply chain; the company has made efforts to reduce its contribution to the waste stream. [122] Additionally, a regenerative septic system recycles wastewater, allowing the company to use only one-third of its annual allotment from the county water district.

Tamper-evident packaging is used to protect the quality of the products and to provide consumers convenience and safety. Recycled cardboard and paper goods are used in packaging and the tea bags are made with unbleached Manila hemp.

According to Kellison, 90% of TM's ingredients are organic and 85% come from outside the US. TM doesn't 'spot buy' ingredients on the open market. Instead, in order to maintain and assure quality, the company has developed long-term equitable relationships with its trading partners. "It's taken us three decades to get to the point where we have a reliable organic supply chain. We did it by working with and investing in our trading partners," said Kellison. [123]

Most of the teas made by Traditional Medicinals contain pharmacopoeial-grade herbs. In 1978, the company began to collaborate with herb growers and wild collectors to increase the availability of organic and

---

[120] Presentation to Sonoma State University students. September 14, 2010

[121] Presentation to Sonoma State EMBA students Feb 6, 2010

[122] Kellison February 6, 2010

[123] Kellison February 6, 2010

pharmacopoeial-grade medicinal herbs. Currently the company has converted over 90% of the herbs it uses to organic.

Some of these herbs can only be grown in very few locations in the world. Because of this, their supply chain can present quite a challenge. Traditional Medicinals works with local growers and with organizations such as the Fair Trade Labeling Organization and the FairWild Foundation to help improve community resources, quality of life, educational opportunities and so on. Both the Fair Trade and FairWild systems have various social and environmental standards that must be met. A premium is also paid above and beyond what the usual cost of an herb might be, and these premiums go into a fund that the communities can use to enhance their quality of life.

Nevertheless, it is a complex system that has taken Traditional Medicinals many years to develop. As Josef Brinckmann, Traditional Medicinals' Vice President for Research and Development, explained to Anna Soref of New Hope 360, "The vast majority of botanicals in commerce are not farmed, they are wild collected. This tradition of wild collection is changing. All over the world, young people are leaving remote rural areas and going to urban areas. The average collector is now between 50 and 90 years old. Unless there is a way for people to make most, or all, of their income from wild collection to support their families, the tradition of wild collecting will come to a stop. We've found that it's not enough to just pay the fair trade premiums; we have to engage even deeper. So in a fair trading system, a company can't really be buying anonymously off the open market; it really requires investment and relationship building—that's the sustainable model. For example, we schedule periodic visits to see what we can do collaboratively that would improve the quality of life for the communities we purchase from, to let them know that we are interested in working very closely together. The way the FairWild system works is that the collectors themselves and then the collection organization and then the final buyer collaboratively discuss each year what the extra monies will be used for to benefit the community."[124]

---

[124] http://newhope360.com/herbal/fair-trade-botanical-supplements-save-dying-tradition-help-families retrieved October 17, 2011

One might wonder whether fair trade protects the environment? Brinckmann says, "Some certifications do and others don't, so you have to look at each standard. FairWild links ecological, economical and sociological sustainability; so in that case, the wild selection has to be proven sustainable through resource assessment, monitoring and management, and there has to be evidence that all of the fair trade principles are handled as well. Our belief is that a prerequisite to ecological sustainability is social sustainability; you can't really separate people, plants and nature. In other words, to implement an ecological sustainability standard like organic without social sustainability is not sustainable."[125]

All Traditional Medicinals' raw materials are rigorously inspected on arrival in the Sebastopol, California factory and subject to strict quality control by the company's quality control lab. Additional quality control testing is done by independent third party laboratories.

TM Foundation and Community Development

The company has established the Traditional Medicinals Foundation to work towards community development in its source communities. Sadler says, "It may appear that we are in the herb business, but really we are in the business of change. We are changing the standards of quality for herbal products, changing the practice of alternative medicine, changing the health of the people who consume our products and changing the lives of the rural native people who farm and collect our herbs in the wild." [126]

Brinckmann adds, "With fair trade they are guaranteed consistent business at minimum fair trade prices, plus a guarantee of investment in their communities. So, it's not so much moving from exploitation to non-exploitation. It's moving from situations of poverty to situations where we can improve the quality of life in the village. For example, say people spend a certain amount of time every day going to get water, but now [fair trade monies] have been invested in water catchment or a well, so people don't have to

---

125 http://newhope360.com/herbal/fair-trade-botanical-supplements-save-dying-tradition-help-families retrieved October 17, 2011
126 www.traditionalmedicinals.com

spend hours getting water every day anymore, so quality of life is improved."[127]

Taking Care of Employees

Donna Nilsen, Senior Accountant at Traditional Medicinals, worked as a CPA for five years until she found herself wanting more out of a job: "I wanted to work for a company with high moral standards." Answering an ad for a position in the company's accounting department, she took the job because, as she puts it, "I finally found a company whose product I could be proud of and that sustains my happiness. I like the way we work at Traditional Medicinals—everything is collaborative. For example, in accounting we work together with operations and human resources to solve problems." [128]

In 2008 the company became an independent, employee-owned company (ESOP) with employees owning a share of the business. According to Kellison this was done in part to preserve the company's mission. Employees who have a stake in the company's future will be more likely to adhere to the company's values and mission than shareholders. "Sustainability has to be the way you do business; this is the only way we can have a business on the planet 50, 100 or 200 years from now." [129]

Judith Yera, Human Resources Manager, started as a temporary employee. The company supported her in completing her BS degree. One of the things she likes about the company is that all 115 employees participate in the company's ESOP and are given shares paid for out of the company's profits.

---

[127] http://newhope360.com/herbal/fair-trade-botanical-supplements-save-dying-tradition-help-families retrieved October 17, 2011
[128] Presentation to Sonoma State University students. September 14, 2010
[129] Kellison February 6, 2010

TM's Business Model

Kellison explains that continuous improvement is an essential element in the company's operation. Profit and growth are an integral part of the company.

In 2010 the company brought in a team of consultants to help them to improve their marketing and operations. Through a focus group they gained a better grasp on how customers think about tea and how best to reach them. They also improved their metrics in keeping careful records of production, order fill rates and on-time shipment for each of their products. This gave them the information needed to determine which of their many tea products were profitable and which were not.

One issue that came up was pricing of products to meet the added costs associated with FairWild's certification. Trish Blue, Controller, explained, "We want customers to pay a responsible price: one that sustains the environment where our products are produced. For that reason our prices are higher than many traditional teas."[130]

Traditional Medicinals respects and strives to support each stakeholder throughout the entire supply chain, from their concentration on collector/cultivator well-being to their alliances with specific distributors, and from partnerships with altruistic causes to renewable energy implementation.

As Lily Thompson, Traditional Medicinals' Brand Steward and Storyteller, explained "Part of our leadership and our modeling of what sustainable business can be, I think, comes from our willingness to honestly address the issues and not shy away from what's difficult or what's imperfect about it all.. Doing good is not so cut and dry or easy to accomplish. And yet, we continually strive to do good, to be a force of well-being wherever we go, whether that is into the homes of our consumers or around the world where we source our herbs."[131]

---

[130] Presentation to Sonoma State University students. September 14, 2010
[131] Lily Thompson personal communication October 12, 2011.

In recognition of its work the company has received a number of awards, including the Community Approach to Sustainability Award presented by the California State Senate and S.E.E. Green in recognition of its commitment to sustainable environmental business practices.

Sustainable and Profitable

A basic tenet of sustainability, according to the company, is the ability to continue to invest in all of the stakeholders of the company. Rather than following a typical corporate business model, in which the ultimate goal is to create value for the shareholders (those few who hold stock in the company), Traditional Medicinals aims to create value for all of its stakeholders, including the people who cultivate and collect the herbs, the communities in which the company operates, its business partners and its employees. The only way to create this value at every touch point is to maintain profitability. As a result of the company's financial success it has been able to allocate approximately $1 million each year to the company's ESOP and still fund community development projects in source communities. Traditional Medicinals is yet another company that looks at sustainability as a way of business.

CHAPTER 10

INDIGENOUS

When it is very cold, there are two ways to warm yourself. One is by putting on a fur coat, the other is by lighting a fire. What is the difference? The difference is that the fur coat warms only the person wearing it, while the fire warms anyone who comes close.[132]

Consider the concept of global trade, with global producers, suppliers, and buyers. Further consider the global supply chain, in which the laborers making the products or growing the crops are often paid the least. The concept of fair trade emerged more than 50 years ago in the US with Ten Thousand Villages, Oxfam Trading in the United Kingdom and the Max Havelaar label in the Netherlands: the idea that we should consider the people who produce the products we buy. Fair trade principles say that trade should create sustainable incomes for producers around the world: wages paid should be fair, working conditions, safe. Businesses play an enormous role in whether trade is fair by compensating producers so that their families can live productive and sustainable lives—or not. California-based INDIGENOUS is one company that has said "yes" to, and built a working model for, fair trade.[133]

---

[132] http://www.sikhchic.com/faith/daya_compassion_one_is_made_of_many

[133] The company was known as Indigenous Designs until 2012 when it changed its name to INDIGENOUS.

Seeds for the business were sown in 1993, when Scott Leonard was selling surfboards in Santa Cruz, California. His soccer buddy Joe Flood walked in wearing a multicolored sweater, which impressed Leonard. "You know, I could sell something like that in my shop!" he exclaimed. His friend said that the sweaters were made by women eking out a living high in the Andes of Ecuador. A month later, Leonard joined Flood on a trip to his native Ecuador to visit small knitting cooperatives. "We literally walked the pavement in a lot of these mountain towns, trying to figure out where and how we could help these people who were often forced to trade their clothing products for food because they could not afford basic necessities," said Leonard.[134]

The knitters used poor quality wool and old bicycle spokes as knitting needles, and makeshift tools for carding and spinning the wool. Lacking access to distribution channels, they walked hours to the nearest village, where they would sell their sweaters, which lacked uniformity in size and even sleeve length, for a fraction of what they were worth. The weavers' inability to access quality fabrics, designs, and tools kept most of them in a perpetual poverty-stricken state.

What Leonard saw in Ecuador bothered him. The peasants' poverty gnawed at him. A desire to relieve that bother, and to end that gnawing, is what ultimately drove the launch of INDIGENOUS. "We had a vision to make a difference in the world; we wanted to have a positive influence on the indigenous women of the Andes," said Leonard. "We decided if we could develop viable designs, control the colors, control the sizing, and put some other quality controls in place, we could market to the outdoor industry and in turn pay these women a sustainable wage." [135]

After he formed the company, Leonard mailed a catalog of the woven clothing with the help of a friend who had worked at Esprit, an international apparel manufacturer. Despite the helpful apparel manufacturing insight, getting the company going proved a challenge. Leonard's initial breakthrough came at Magic, the fashion and clothing industry's annual trade show in Las Vegas.

---

[134] Pride Scott Wright from greensteps.org. http://www.greensteps.org/stepone/indigenousdesigns.htm.
[135] http://www.greensteps.org/stepone/indigenousdesigns.htm.

The show had not been going particularly well when Leonard happened to see the Nature Company crew walking by. He got their attention, set up an appointment and, ultimately, ended up with a purchase order for over $450,000. INDIGENOUS committed to deliver 4,000 sweaters and 2,000 jackets—a great start for the foundling company.

But there were problems. Could the women meet the Nature Company's exacting quality standards? Could they deliver the order on time? The weavers were loosely organized into cooperatives, and Leonard was having difficulty getting the co-ops to produce the promised items on time. At the wedding of a mutual friend, Leonard ran into Matt Reynolds, a high school friend who had lived in Ecuador and who had just returned from several years working with a large retailer in Europe. In 1995, Reynolds joined the firm as partner and immediately set off for Ecuador to get production on track.[136]

Among his chief challenges: How to standardize production among a group of cooperatives? Working with non-governmental organizations (NGOs), the company created a set of prototype clothing samples. Then, cooperatives selected their best knitters to train other knitters. INDIGENOUS also provided free, 10-day knitting workshops, which trained the women in the importance of sizing and color, how to follow patterns and designs, how to work with a wider variety of yarns, and the value of quality control.

Reynolds contacted the director of each of the co-ops. "We're going to give you two thousand sweaters to knit," he said. He wrote into the agreement that if one of the three co-ops failed to produce all two thousand units, one of the others had to cover the shortfall.

The firm's first order from the Nature Company was a breakthrough in many ways. Until this point, the small cooperatives were competing among themselves. But with that large an order, no single group could fulfill it alone. The three co-ops had to work together. "When they completed the work and received payment, a light bulb went on. It showed the women that they could do better by cooperating among themselves," explained Reynolds.

---

[136] This information and quotations that follow come from personal interviews with Matt Reynolds.

In contacting the weavers Reynolds's approach was not "We'll help you," but "What you are doing is amazing! We can bring you some new fibers and teach you how to make a sweater that sells for more than you could imagine and it won't cost you anything, you won't have to leave your village, and you can still keep your farm and grow your crops."[137]

As the women completed the training and began receiving increased payments for their products, they began to realize that their products had value on the world market. They also began to see opportunities for advancement that had never occurred to them before, such as opportunities to become trainers in the expanding network of weavers. The women also began to see real returns within their communities and families as more money flowed in to pay for the education of their children.

A Quadruple Bottom Line?

Despite this early success, INDIGENOUS was still riddled with challenges. Leonard and Reynolds were savvy enough to know that if they wanted to fulfill their goal of helping others, then their company had to be fiscally sound and prosperous. Without economic sustainability, they knew, all other goals would be short-lived.

To create the sustainability they were after, the two decided that Indigenous would be a quadruple bottom line company. What does this mean? Most companies seek to maximize profitability—a single bottom line—not considering how operations impact other "bottom lines," such as the environment or the community. A growing number of companies are "triple bottom line" companies, having added to their objectives ecological stewardship and impact on employees and the local community. Leonard and Reynolds, since they were partnering with organizations around the world to help improve economic and social conditions, wanted to go a step beyond that, also considering the company's global impact.

Despite the worthy goal of becoming a quadruple bottom line company, Leonard and Reynolds still had a mountain to climb to consistently get quality product from the cooperatives. They also had to grow or find a

---

[137] Matt Reynolds presentation to EMBA cohort 1. Dec 11, 2010.

sizable market that extended beyond the Nature Company; they would also need at least $300,000 to take the venture to the next level. The entrepreneurs were able to piece together start-up funding from personal savings, loans from family and friends, and a $200,000 loan from the US Small Business Association. The new inflow of funding enabled the firm to begin partnering with artisans through local cooperatives, and to produce, inspect, transport, and sell small orders to retailers.

A Credit Crisis

However, just when the company began contacting the cooperatives to place orders, they discovered yet another problem: the co-ops lacked the financial resources for anything but tiny orders; they could not purchase the materials or sustain themselves. As Reynolds put it "When we hit one million dollars in sales we hit a wall." The company was strapped for cash since it could take up to 180 days before it received payment for cash advances to artisan producers. Some of the cooperatives were working with NGOs, which provided microloans to the tune of about $100—insufficient working capital for the size of the orders.

The answer: extend credit to the co-ops. But this was not a sustainable solution, as extending credit caused INDIGENOUS to exhaust its own start-up capital by 1999. "We were maxed out," explained Reynolds. "Interest costs were killing us. Traditional banks and financial institutions wouldn't lend to us." The hand-knit cooperatives were still viewed as high risk by traditional banks because the co-ops could not offer the collateral required for a traditional loan. As a result, sales flattened; Indigenous was stretched to the breaking point.

Root Capital to the Rescue

The solution came from another innovative company, Root Capital, founded by Willie Fulbright Foote, grandson of the late US Senator James William Fulbright, well known for his Fulbright fellowship program. Foote established Root Capital to promote the conservation of natural resources in rural areas of Latin America,[138] as well as to provide a vehicle for loans to small and medium firms dedicated to exporting "green" products, such as fair trade coffee and other sustainably produced goods.

Root Capital sees the key to transforming rural poverty as promoting sustainable livelihoods that affirm local cultures and strengthen community participation in natural resource management. Lending money to INDIGENOUS would help the women weavers to define new economic opportunities while promoting the local stewardship of regionally and globally important resources. And, by providing affordable loans and financial services to social businesses, Root Capital could also support an environmentally sustainable company, one that would otherwise have difficulty obtaining traditional loans.

Though the financing issue had been resolved, Leonard and Reynolds hit yet another obstacle. The loan from Root Capital required that the cooperatives pay interest before receiving payment for their goods. This concept was foreign to the women. How could INDIGENOUS get the women to understand that they needed to pay interest on their loans until the customer paid for the product? Working closely with Root Capital, Reynolds developed a workshop series to show the cooperatives how earnings from increased production would pay the interest and still leave more money. Crossing this barrier moved the company to another plateau. As a result, business grew by a whopping 93 percent over the next year.

INDIGENOUS invested more than seven million dollars in Peru, Ecuador, Guatemala, and India to train and educate artisans, build cooperative work centers, provide design expertise, and set up logistics. Scaling has allowed the firm to supply larger, mainstream companies, such as Dillard's department stores and the clothing retailer Eileen Fisher.[139]

---

[138] In 1996, Root Capital was known as EcoLogic Finance. Considered too small and risky for mainstream banks and too large for microfinance, grassroots businesses cannot access the capital they need to grow and sustain their operations. Root Capital addresses this market failure through its innovative lending model.

[139] Although the clothes are completely hand knit, Indigenous Designs also owns key patents for their clothing designs. Their name brand is becoming increasingly recognizable in the organic and fair trade industry, synonymous with fair labor prices and quality products. These may provide additional advantages to the company over potential competitors. Nevertheless, just how important sustainability is in the market is not entirely clear.

Indigenous developed ties with more than 275 cooperatives of six to sixty people. This added capacity allows the firm to produce a high volume of hand-knit garments.[140]

The time, money, and resources the company poured into infrastructure yielded dividends, both for the company and the communities; Reynolds estimates that for every dollar they invested paid about $20 in benefits to the community. But moreover, the unique relationship with local people allows the firm to build trust and acceptance, which translates into competitive advantage.

By following fair-trade practices and paying a livable wage, INDIGENOUS helps thousands of artisans and their families rise out of poverty. The company partners with non-profits and government agencies to provide family educational assistance, flexible work hours, and opportunities for promotion. Indigenous also provides free knitting needles and assistance in financing new equipment such as looms, while company-financed work centers allow artisans to knit together and avoid long walks to the nearest large city to sell their individual products.

A Business Model with Results

INDIGENOUS has profited handsomely from its model. Through 2008, the company experienced double-digit annual growth as the value of its initial investment grew 20 times. With the onset of the worldwide economic downturn, sales within the US clothing industry plummeted by 25 percent, leading some of the company's competitors to file for bankruptcy or to suffer losses. Yet because of the goodwill generated over its years of work, and because of the diversity of its supplier network, INDIGENOUS maintained its operations without a decline in sales.

Indigenous ensures that its artisans are paid a fair value for their work. Indigenous pays artisans who produce for the firm a 15 to 30 per cent

---

[140] This capacity continues to grow as word spreads within the indigenous people community of the opportunities to be had by working for a fair-trade company. By offering fair-trade wages, Indigenous Designs can continue to increase the number and size of the cooperatives it works with, thus growing production capacity and increasing speed. Large capacity allows the firm to take advantage of economies of scale, resulting in lower per-unit costs to produce, inspect, and ship each garment.

premium over employees who work for other employers in large cities . Because it has stayed true to its principles, the company has achieved profitability and sustained earnings even through a recession. The company pursues ecological stewardship by using natural, organic, and sustainable raw materials that are not harmful to the environment. It partners with organizations around the world to help provide education and fair-trade and organic certifications, while also providing access to incomes and financing for indigenous people to enable self-support. INDIGENOUS' website lists impressive stories of artisans who have improved their lives— the stories that sustain the company and its efforts. In 2008, the firm became a founding B Corporation, cementing its commitment to global social justice and environmental stewardship, and its place in our roster of good companies. [141]

---

[141] www.indigenous.com

CHAPTER 11
ARAVIND EYE CARE AND AUROLAB

He felt the joy of others as his joy.
He felt the grief of others as his grief.
SRI AUROBINDO

Some enterprises are driven by a mission to produce goods or services for a social purpose; benefiting society's disadvantaged. A variety of such organizations are emerging daily to combine the energies of social concern with the logic of the marketplace to meet the needs of millions worldwide.[142] Aravind Eye Care has developed an efficient business model to treat blindness in India inexpensively and on a large scale performing more than two million surgeries a year using intraocular lenses, products made through its partner business, Aurolab.

Aravind founder, Dr. G. Venkataswamy, grew up in southern India where blindness is endemic and widespread and asked himself "How can I give the poor man back his sight, how can I eradicate all of this unnecessary blindness?" In India a blind man is like a mouth without hands. Dr. V began by performing thousands of cataract surgeries on his own.

"Dr. V. came to the conclusion as a young man that "intelligence and capability are not enough. There must be the joy of doing something

---

142 See Paul Hawken's book Blessed Unrest. Viking Books. 2007. The New Heroes

beautiful." So instead of retiring at the age of 65, Dr. V. mortgaged his home and opened a hospital to perform free or low-cost cataract surgery—if untreated cataracts can lead to blindness—on poor Indians. In his first year, Dr. V. performed 5000 surgeries." [143]

But he could scarcely make a dent in the number of sightless people. His solution was to develop a social enterprise combining western capitalism with Eastern spiritualism. From the West he took the assembly line model of Henry Ford and McDonald's to keep costs low and generate a profit. From the East he took the principle of spiritual service applying the profits earned to help the poor. "My goal was to see how many people we could help; more money earned then more people served." He developed a model of compassionate capitalism. "Profit is a means to an end, not an end in itself."

A Mission to Eradicate Blindness

Aravind Eye Care, one of the most successful and admired enterprises in India, has a mission to eradicate unnecessary blindness. Aravind had its start as an 11-bed hospital operated by Dr. G. Venkataswamy.

Beginning in the southern India state of Tamil Nadu, Dr. V. focused on innovations in the workflow, applying advanced managerial concepts to minimize the per patient cost of treatment and post operative care. Aravind has since grown to a world-class eye care system of clinics, institutes and manufacturing centers. The system began its work under the nonprofit Govel Trust and by 2003 had grown into The Aravind Eye Care System, comprising a chain of five hospitals where they perform cataract surgeries and insert intraocular lenses (IOLs). The Trust added a center for manufacturing lenses in order to reduce the cost of one of the main sources of expense. It also operates institutes for eye care training, research, and programs for community outreach. Together by the end of 2011 the five Aravind Eye

---

[143] www.pbs.org/opb/thenewheroes retrieved Feb 14, 2011.

hospitals have seen over 32 million patients and performed more than 4 million surgeries.[144]

Aravind's Model

Due to Aravind's pioneering business model, the majority of surgeries are free and Aravind is financially self-supporting. By charging wealthier patients more and poorer patients less, it has been able to provide quality care at a very low cost. Dr. V says "In running our business we ask what is the least amount we can charge and still survive?"

The rates charged by Aravind are modest; besides the free patients who are treated in 'eye camps' with aid from government grants and donations, there are several choices available to fee paying patients depending on the category of elective surgery and accommodations they choose. In addition, tight financial controls, use of a large paramedical staff (who are recruited and trained by Aravind) and an assembly line workflow keep costs in a range of $50 to $330 per patient.[145]

Aravind's innovative community outreach programs include Eye Camps, eye screening of school children, and IT tele-advice kiosks. Aravind organizes about 1,500 eye camps each year conducted with sponsorship and assistance from NGOs like the Rotary or Lions Club, local industrialists and government. The camps gather patients, test them and conduct any necessary surgeries on the spot. With Sight Savers International, they sponsor a project to rehabilitate persons considered incurably blind while building skills and community support. Each year Aravind screens thousands of school children and trains teachers to identify signs of visual deficiency. In one of the most innovative projects, launched in partnership with the Indian Institute of Technology, kiosks were put up all over Tamil Nadu fitted out with web-cameras that enable patients to take a picture of their eyes and send them as an email along with a voice description of the problem to an Aravind doctor. The doctor makes a diagnosis and gives advice to the patient. By 2011 Aravind was running 36 vision centers that

---

[144] Pavithra Mehta and Suchitra Shenoy. Infinite Vision. Berrett-Koehler, 2011 and CK Prahalad. The Fortune at the Bottom of the Pyramid. Wharton School Publishing. 2005. pp.265-286
[145] Prahalad, 2005.

collectively process over 550 telemedicine consultations every day at a fee of less than 50 cents.

Aurolab

As Aravind's surgeries grew so did its demand for intraocular lenses. In 1990 Aravind set its sights on reducing the cost of IOLs from between $80 and $150 per lens and seeking to produce them at an affordable price. Seva Foundation's David Green began working along with Dr. Bala Krishnan to meet this challenge. Seva's Suzanne Gilbert summarized the challenge "We were told we were crazy and that the plan wouldn't work. That it could never happen outside the U.S., Europe, and Australia. That India's heat, dirt, erratic electricity, and low worker productivity would compromise our efforts."[146] With assistance from several foundations including Seva Foundation, Sight Savers International and CIDA in 1992 Aurolab, named after Sri Aurobindo, began operation. By 2002 Aurolab was able to get the cost down to less than $4. Demand for the company's products exploded; by 2009 Aurolab was producing more than 2 million lenses per year.

The company's mission statement is, "Eliminating needless blindness by making high quality ophthalmic products affordable and accessible to vision impaired worldwide". They have successfully become the world's second largest manufacturer of cataract lenses and remained financially stable generating revenues of thirty percent above their expenses. The sale of hearing aids and lenses to upper-middle class patients generate profits to offset their losses from the sales to poor people. Aravind's goal is for every one patient that can afford to pay funds the subsidized treatment of two additional patients and all of the growth and expansion projects they have planned.

Aurolab's innovative approach has had far reaching impact; driving down prices of intraocular lenses all over the world and spreading its model of compassionate capitalism. Traditional enterprises earn profits for the few owners and feed a few mouths; social enterprises use their profits to feed many mouths. Aurolab sells its products at the lowest cost it can in order to

---

[146] Pavithra Mehta and Suchitra Shenoy. Infinite Vision. Berrett-Koehler, 2011 p. 153

survive. Profit is seen as a means to an end, helping as many people as they can.

Dr. V and the team at Aravind are convinced that western style capitalism has failed to grasp opportunities in the developing world because of a focus on extracting the highest possible profit from every item sold. Their conception of "compassionate capitalism" extracts a small amount of profit from each item sold, but generates a high sales volume thereby making it possible to make available critical goods and services, like eye care, to billions of people around the world. As David Green says "Profit is a means to an end, not an end in itself." Meanwhile, Dr. V. draws his inspiration from the Eastern spiritual leader Sri Aurobindo. "The job of each human being" he says "is to experience the divine and then use what one has learned to serve others."

As Robert Redford observed in his New Heroes public television series "Dr. V. and David Green have made medical technology and health care services accessible, affordable and financially self-sustaining. Aurolab's products are used by eye care institutions and ophthalmologists in more than 120 countries. The factory produces hundreds of thousands of lenses each year—10 percent of the world supply—at $5.00 a pair. The company turns a profit of thirty percent on its investment. With the revenue stream produced by Aurolab, Dr. V. has been able to open five new eye hospitals in southern India. Through Aravind Eye Hospital and Aurolab, Dr. V. and David Green have performed what might as well be miracles for elderly Indians living in remote villages. Restoring their sight and hearing has given them back their dignity and allowed them to contribute to their communities again." [147]

A study prepared by researchers from the University of California concluded "This socially-driven organization produces ophthalmic technologies more cost effectively than any other comparable manufacturer, delivering their products to over 120 countries and owning 10 percent of the global market for intraocular lenses."[148] The lenses meet and often

---

[147] The New Heroes

[148] Jaspal Sandhu et.al. "Appropriate Design of Medical Technologies for Developing Regions: The Case of Aurolab." November 2005. Quoted in Mehta and Shenoy., p. 156

exceed the standards of US and European producers and received International Standard Office certification for quality.

Aravind's Results

Aravind succeeds because its business model is built on compassion. Pavithra Mehta and Suchitra Shenoy make the case that Aravind's 'upside-down' business model of not turning anyone away and not compromising on the quality of care was an essential component of its remarkable success both socially as well as financially. Dr. V consistently steered the company to make improvements and adopt new practices not to maximize revenues and profits but rather "to see how much we can give with the resources we have." By setting its sights on making professional eye care easy, accessible and affordable, Aravind has provided high quality care regardless of the patient's capacity to pay. In fact one quarter of surgeries are provided entirely free of charge, another quarter are provided for a minimal payment of between $11 and $17 while the remaining half of all patients pay a market rate of between $111 and $1044. Aravind's business model is all the more remarkable since in 2010 the enterprise earned a $13 million surplus on revenues of $29 million.[149]

---

[149] Pavithra Mehta and Suchitra Shenoy. Infinite Vision. Berrett-Koehler, 2011

CHAPTER 12
KIVA.ORG

Meet Godfrey Kalyango. Godfrey, his wife, and three children live in Kampala, Uganda. He is 28 years old, and earns a living selling sugar and other staples from a small retail store. To help expand his business enough to increase profits and to continue to pay school fees for his children, Godfrey needs to invest more in his business—he needs a loan of $750 USD.

Meet Rohat, a wife and mother of three children in Tajikistan. Rohat is in the bakery business, cooking bread and selling it in her local market. To expand her business, Rohat needs a loan of $1,900 USD, which she will use to buy flour and coal.

Meet my granddaughter Ariel, who lives in Albany, California. Ariel (and tens of thousands like her around the world) regularly logs-in to Kiva.org to browse the profiles of entrepreneurs like Godfrey and Rohat, lending $25 or $50 directly to support their specific entrepreneurial initiatives. Over the course of her loans, Ariel receives regular email updates on her borrowers' repayments. Then, when her loans are repaid, she browses portfolios again, viewing "risk ratings" and delinquency and default rates, and then relending her funds to others in need.

The service Ariel uses is www.kiva.org , the world's first person-to-person micro-lending website. Micro-lenders, like Ariel, generally provide very small loans to collectives and individuals unable to receive credit from traditional or mainstream financial institutions. Micro- lending websites, like Kiva, bring micro-lenders and individuals needing loans, like Godfrey and Rohat, together.

Although the idea of bringing diverse, worldwide groups of individual lenders and borrowers together via an online platform is new, the concept of micro-finance is not. Informal savings and credit groups have operated for centuries, providing informal credit when and as needed.[150] Formal savings institutions have also long provided financial services to customers otherwise traditionally neglected, either because small borrowers lacked collateral, or because the amounts needed were regarded as too small to be profitable.[151]

A new wave of interest in micro-finance hit in the 1970s with experimental programs by individuals like Nobel Prize winner Mohammed Yunus, founder of the Grameen Bank in Bangladesh, and in Brazil by Accion, which, to invest in micro-businesses, extended loans of less than $1,000 to groups of poor women. Such programs generally focused on providing credit for income-generating activities and targeted very poor and mainly women borrowers. These micro-finance experiments not only showed the power of business to transform the lives of the poor, but also that impoverished borrowers become empowered to find solutions to a range of problems and issues as they learn to operate in the marketplace.

This new wave of micro-credit programs also established that poor people, especially women, had excellent repayment rates—rates far better than those in the formal financial sectors of most developing countries. These same programs also established that the key to early micro- credit program success was that every member of a group guaranteed the repayment of every other member.

---

[150] These include the "susus" of Ghana, "chit funds" in India, "tandas" in Mexico, "arisan" in Indonesia, "tontines" in West Africa, and "pasanaku" in Bolivia, as well as numerous savings clubs and burial societies found all over the world. See www.networkers.org/userfiles/The%20History%20of%20Microfinance.doc

[151] Some early micro credit organization which provided small loans to rural poor in with no collateral during the 18th century were the Irish Loan Fund and a variety of savings and credit institutions in Europe organized primarily among the rural and urban poor known as People's Banks, Credit Unions, and Savings and Credit Co-operatives.

Kiva's Unique Business Model

Similarly, Kiva acts as a backing bank of sorts, enabling micro-finance institutions (MFIs) to raise debt capital directly from individual and group social investors via the Internet. Kiva partners with existing MFIs around the world equipped with expertise in choosing qualified entrepreneurs in their local regions so that the money goes to individuals and groups in need and armed with viable business plans. Kiva provides interest-free, US-dollar loans to these partners, who then lend to entrepreneurs and agree to comply with transparency on the Internet. MFIs, in turn, lend this infused capital at prevailing in-country interest rates and keep the interest income. Losses arising from client default are borne by the people, like my granddaughter, who lend through Kiva.

Named as one of the top ideas in 2006 by the New York Times Magazine, Kiva's innovation is its data-rich, transparent lending platform, which shows the social investors or individual lenders around the world how their money flows through the entire loan cycle, and what effect their loans have on the people and institutions lending, borrowing, and managing them, all the while tapping the power of the Internet to facilitate the one-to-one connections that used to be prohibitively expensive. In contrast with the business of child sponsorship, known for its high overhead, Kiva creates interpersonal connections at much lower costs due to instant, inexpensive Internet delivery. Also, by sharing its technology with partners—existing MFIs such as World Relief in Cambodia and Pro Mujer in Bolivia—Kiva gains access to potential entrepreneurs from impoverished communities without needing to place staff on the ground in remote locations, and gets MFIs to do the work of uploading and maintaining entrepreneur profiles for lenders around the world to peruse.

Getting Started

But what is now seemingly effortless "doing good" through the power of the Internet was not without its bumps and stalls. Kiva.org was born in 2004 while Jessica Jackley was working writing case studies about villagers in Africa for the Village Enterprise Fund. A few months later, her husband, Matt Flannery joined her; as they rode a bus down bumpy roads in Africa they thought about ways to improve the lot of the villagers they were meeting. Flannery was working as a computer programmer for TiVo; Jackley worked at the Stanford Business School, where both had heard Dr. Mohammed Yunus—founder of the Grameen Bank in Bangladesh—speak on the topic of micro-finance. Inspired by their experience, the couple created a plan for people-to people lending. "I reacted with both my head and my heart," Jackley recalls. "My head said: 'Microfinance is effective. It's powerful. It works.' But the most important part was what my heart said. The way he talked about the poor was beautiful, respectful, and dignified. I didn't have feelings of guilt and shame like I did after a lot of nonprofit messaging. Instead, I wanted to be there, listening to people's stories and talking with clients face to face."[152]

They pitched their idea to Geoff Davis, CEO of Unitus, a "micro-finance accelerator" who pointed out two challenges in the plan: (1) the difficulty of creating a scalable business, and (2) the high costs of connecting one lender to one borrower so that borrowers might see where their money was going. The team pressed ahead anyway, running into even more challenges surrounding incorporation and tax status. At that point, they decided to "just start," and see where things went.

The couple spent the first few months of 2005 developing a beta version of the website, choosing Kiva, which means "unity," as its name. They emailed 300 friends from their wedding invitation list asking for help, and ended up raising $3,500 to get Kiva off the ground.

Soon, friends started calling to ask how their loans were doing. Matt Flannery recalled "Our first real success story was a fish seller in Uganda named Elizabeth Omalla. 'Hey, did you hear?' one friend called to tell me, 'Elizabeth sold twice as much fish this week with the money we loaned to her!' Since Kiva began providing her loans, Elizabeth is now able to take her children to school, buy two cows and five goats and open a savings account."[153]

Inspired by this early success, Flannery and Jackley prepared a 40-page business plan and started talking with micro-finance professionals, United

---

[152] http://www.ssireview.org/articles/entry/the_profit_in_nonprofit/
[153] Quoted in Wilford Welch. Tactics of Hope. P.90-91

Nations' experts, and international lawyers. The advice they received from these 'experts' was that their concept wouldn't work. "They said our idea would not scale," explained Flannery. "They said the overhead would cripple the cash flow margin. And ...that Kiva was too much like other child sponsorship organizations. It was all very disheartening."[154]

But then came several big breaks. First, Premal Shah joined their team. Shah worked at eBay and brought with him eBay's support, a key to Kiva's success since eBay donates free payment processing. Second, Kiva was featured in a blog on the Daily Kos home page. That feature, read by more than one million people, resulted in more than 1,000 emails and an infusion of $10,000.

Nevertheless, near the end of 2006, Kiva was still not generating enough funds to stay afloat. Then, on Halloween night, came an answer to the couple's prayers: a 15-minute segment on Public Television's Frontline about Kiva sent their volume skyrocketing overnight—from $3,000 per day to $30,000 per day. Before the show aired, Kiva had processed a total of $500,000 in loans. Seven months after the show, that figure jumped to more than $5.5 million.

How Kiva Works[155]

Individuals located anywhere in the world interested in lending to another individual need only follow a few simple steps. First, lenders browse a list of profiles of entrepreneurs in need, sorting and exploring by gender, sector (agriculture, education, health), region, or loan terms—a granularity that gives lenders the ability to pinpoint exactly where their money goes. This specificity in charitable giving differs greatly from giving to other large organizations that simply collect funds for broad purposes and then decide internally how and where to disperse funds. Once lenders identify entrepreneurs of interest, they may read their profiles to get more information.

---

[154] Welch. P. 91
[155] Source: www.kiva.org

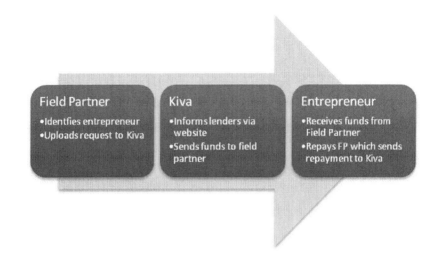

Figure 12.1 How Kiva Works

For example, Semmatimba Florence is a 45-year-old widow who knows her back would be against the wall had she not taken the initiative to blaze a business trail seven years ago. She began as a worker in a stone quarry while trying to come to grips with the death of her husband, who had been the family's sole breadwinner. In the years that followed, Florence lived by her wits. Sensing that she was having difficulty providing for her family, a close friend persuaded Florence to bear a hand in any business activity that could extricate her from her predicament. It was then that this cheerful mother of eight tried stone quarrying. With time, she changed her priorities and began a restaurant and hotel business in Kilangira-Mukono. Her stone quarry business, however, is something over which she still reigns. And she has never looked back. In a week, Florence makes profits that sum to 100,000 shillings. With this loan, she will buy more utensils, i.e., cutlery, for her restaurant and equipment for her stone quarrying business. She needs $1,100 and as of August 20, 2010 had raised $825 from 28 lenders scattered around the globe.[156]

---

[156] www.kiva.org retrieved Aug. 20, 2010

Lenders choose to loan to entrepreneurs of their choice in $25 increments up to the full loan amount. On average, it takes only one-and-a-half days for a borrower's loan request to be fully funded.[157] Kiva then wires newly loaned funds to an MFI partner in the entrepreneur's country, who in turn lends the money to the borrower. According to Kiva.org, each field partner must "have a history (at least 2-3 years) of lending to poor, excluded, and/or vulnerable people for the purpose of alleviating poverty or reducing vulnerability; be registered as a legal entity in its country of operation; [and] have at least 1 year of financial audits." [158]

Field partners are responsible for photographing borrowers, writing descriptions of borrowers' businesses, providing updates, and maintaining communication with lenders via the Internet. Because transparency is important to Kiva, field partners are required to report on just how borrowers lives are affected at least once per loan term, and to post such reports on Kiva's website. Along with these responsibilities also come benefits, as field partners, by working with Kiva, they gain positive exposure to a worldwide audience of over 500,000 social investors, low costs including those for staff, administration, and foreign hedging, and zero-percent interest on debt capital.

When lenders are logged in to the Kiva.org website, they see which field partners are associated with their chosen entrepreneurs. For example, lenders see that Christian Rural Aid Network's (CRAN's) mission "is to work towards improvement in the quality of life for the rural poor and disadvantaged populations and communities in a holistic manner (physically, socially, economically and spiritually) with emphasis on the economic and social empowerment of women." Lenders also see that CRAN has been with Kiva for 16 months, has worked with 1,624 entrepreneurs raising a total of $763,950, and has delinquency and default rates of zero percent. Lenders also see that Kiva has awarded CRAN a 4-star (out of 5) rating, indicating that the organization has shown significant reliability in repayment and that Kiva has confidence that the field partner will dutifully administer and collect their loans. When it is time for borrowers to repay their loans in monthly installments, they give the funds

---

[157] www.kiva.org
[158] www.kiva.org retrieved Aug 20,2010

to field partners, who in turn send the money back to the countries from which the funds were originally lent. Loans are set up so that borrowers can repay in monthly installments.

One borrower had this to say about the impact Kiva has had on his life:

" *It's always unbelievable that a poor man's state can change in Africa. Here, people are too poor such that a man like me is considered to be among the poorest of the poor. I thank God for the founders of Kiva who made it possible for me to meet people with big heart for the suffering people of the continent of Africa. I received loan money worth $500 from Kiva almost a year ago. I decided to be very focused on the business that I was running through the support of Village Enterprise Fund grant money worth $100. Before the loan money, I used to buy only one cow and walk with it to the cattle market. This would cost me an amount of 230-250,000 Ugandan shillings. Then sell it at around 270-280,000 Ugandan shillings. Now the profit of 20-30,000 shillings was not enough to meet all our basic needs and then keep the business going well. The whole situation changed when I got a Kiva loan of $500. The first step is that the stock increased from buying only one cow to buying six cows at same time. This caused a great change in our income due to a good amount of money coming in from the profit. Today, I can comfortably buy up to 12 cows and then drive them to cattle market. Our business has grown by 80% ever since we got the loan money. This is the present achievement that I've got from our business:*

1. Renovate our house that was falling a part

2. Buy beddings for myself and my seven Children. At least now each Child has a pair of bed sheets (unbelievable).

3. I can afford a good nutritious food for the family. Our family is able to eat meat twice in a week, fish twice in a week, take tea with sugar for a whole week, (this was not there before).

4. Cater for family treatment, basic essential needs.

5. Now we have our own one cow, two (2) goats, twelve (12) chicken, three (3) turkeys and four (4) piglets.

6. All my Children who had dropped out of school has resumed their studies because now I can afford to pay their school fees and buy scholastic materials for each of them.[sic]"[159]

Today, Kiva's model has been followed by many others in just a few short years. What is unique about Kiva, though, is that Kiva empowers individuals to lend directly to selected entrepreneurs in the developing world in accord with Kiva's mission: to connect people through lending for the sake of alleviating poverty.

Kiva is a non-profit although Jackley and Flannery wanted it to be a for-profit company. However, the regulatory obstacles needed to register the company with the SEC would have been prohibitive.[160] The nonprofit route was the quickest way to get the site up and running. Nevertheless, being a nonprofit has led to many unforeseen benefits including help from PayPal Inc. and YouTube Inc., which bestow donations of their services to Kiva. "Some of the best business and Internet talents in Silicon Valley freely funnel their time and energy to Kiva. And both individual and institutional donors help underwrite the costs of the site."[161]

In addition, lenders are invited to make an optional 10 percent donation to Kiva, in addition to the value of their loan. A donor who makes a $25 loan to a borrower, for example, would be invited to contribute an additional $2.50 to help support Kiva. "In 2008, optional transaction fees totaled $2.2 million... covering some 37 percent of Kiva's operating costs." Flannery adds, "We are building a community based on trust," he says. "We are asking people to concede profit to help a poor person. In turn, Kiva agrees not to profit from people's goodwill. If we did convert to a for-profit model, our users would probably trust us less." A 2006 survey found that half of

---

[159] www.kiva.org retrieved Aug 20,2010

[160] "Kiva's founders originally wanted to offer lenders the option of earning interest on their loans, both to attract lenders and to transform the usual wealthy donor-poor beneficiary hierarchy into the more egalitarian lender- borrower relationship. Yet returning interest on loans could have turned the loan into a security in the eyes of the Securities and Exchange Commission (SEC). Offering a security to the public would trigger a long list of SEC requirements, including sufficiently collateralizing the loans and investing only in entities that comply with U.S. accounting standards."
http://www.ssireview.org/articles/entry/the_profit_in_nonprofit/ retrieved Aug. 24, 2011

[161] http://www.ssireview.org/articles/entry/the_profit_in_nonprofit/ retrieved Aug. 24, 2011

Kiva's lenders "would not lend on the site if it adopted a for-profit model."[162]

Kiva is a non-profit. It does not generate revenues to be distributed to shareholders. What it does is raise money to spread opportunity and generate income earning opportunities for hundreds of thousands of people on five continents. Kiva has generated revenue and profits for its 136 field partners located in 60 countries. Since its inception to September 2011 Kiva raised $241 million and provided 625,000 loans. Women entrepreneurs received 81 percent of the loans; the average loan was $385 and the repayment rate was a remarkable 98.8 percent.

Kiva's audited results for 2007 through 2010 show that the company's revenues exceeded its expenses every single year. In 2010 revenues exceeded expenses by $5.1 million.[163]

---

[162] http://www.ssireview.org/articles/entry/the_profit_in_nonprofit/ retrieved Aug. 24, 2011
[163] www.kiva.org retrieved Sept 15, 2011.

CHAPTER 13
INTERFACE CARPETS

"We know that every natural system on the planet is disintegrating. The land, water, air, and the sea have been functionally transformed from life-supporting systems into repositories for waste. There is no polite way to say that business is destroying the world."

PAUL HAWKEN THE ECOLOGY OF COMMERCE

Paul Hawken's words have shattered the worldview of many an executive, Ray Anderson, CEO of Interface Carpets, among them. "I was convicted of plundering the earth," he said, thinking back to when he first read Hawken's book. "I knew I had to change the way I did business." When your business is a billion-dollar industrial carpet company that manufactures on four continents and services more than 110 locations worldwide, changing the way you operate is, to say the least, a major undertaking.

But change, Interface did. As Anderson tells it, in 1994, at the age of 60, he found himself thinking less about retirement and more about the need for change. "We began to hear this question from customers that we had never heard before...: 'What is your company doing for the environment?'" Anderson said. "We had no answers, it was very embarrassing. It was awkward for our sales people, our manufacturing people, and research people. We didn't have anything to say." [164]

With just an inkling of change on his mental horizon, and to ease his and his team's feeling of being tongue tied, Anderson launched a task force to assess Interface's environmental position.[165] The task force was to gather on August 31, 1994 for its kickoff meeting, which Anderson was expected to open with a speech about the firm's environment vision. "I didn't have an environmental position and I didn't want to make that speech," he said. "I had never given a thought of what we were taking from the earth, doing to the earth, to make our products."

By mid-August, with the date creeping closer, Anderson still didn't know what he would say.

"I couldn't get beyond, 'We obey the law; comply.' And I knew 'comply' was not a vision. And it's in the middle of this that a book lands on my desk, and just by pure serendipity, it's Paul Hawkens' book, The Ecology of Commerce. I had never heard of Paul Hawkens. I didn't know anything about the book; I picked it up not having any idea of what's in it. I start to thumb through it. About page 17, I come to a chapter heading: "The Death of Birth." Whoa... and I started to read. I learned the death of birth is Edwin Wilson's phrase "species extinction," species disappearing never ever to experience the miracle of birth again. Within ten pages, it was a spear in the chest. Just an epiphinal experience. I read that book, I made that speech using Hawkens' material, and I challenged that little group of people who lead our company to sustainability. I was convicted by Hawkens as a plunderer of the earth."[166]

Building Sustainability

At kickoff, Anderson challenged Interface's research group to develop an environmental policy, the result of which was Mission Zero: to reach

---

[164] Ray Anderson on Sustainability. www.youtube.com/watch?v=4bAdsJCHGyU
[165] Ray C. Anderson, Mid-course Correction; Chelsea Green Publishing Company, 1998. p. 39.
[166] Ray Anderson on Sustainability. www.youtube.com/watch?v=4bAdsJCHGyU

sustainability and to become a restorative enterprise (a restorative enterprise being a firm that limits negative effects to the biosphere by using only materials that can be recycled or regenerated). The research group also developed a new, strategic business model based on seven regenerative imperatives: reduce, reuse, reclaim, recycle, redesign, adopt best practices, and challenge suppliers to do the same. Anderson called the firm's new approach the seven faces of "Mount Sustainability," the top of which represents zero impact on the environment. "To climb that mountain and clear the top [means reaching the] point [that] symbolizes zero footprint, zero environmental impact," explained Anderson. "But the first face of the mountain that we tackled was the face of waste. We began to eliminate the very concept of [it]," he said.

Anderson started with the first face, seeking to eliminate waste, even "the very concept of waste," he explained. Eliminating waste meant eliminating scrap and recycling old carpet, giving it new life by using it to create new products—a move that both reduced waste and cut costs. While climbing this first face of Mount Sustainability, Anderson realized just how much money his mission would save. "We began to capture the low-hanging fruit and we racked up savings very, very quickly," said Anderson. "Real savings, dollar and cents savings, and we could go to our shareholders about this, as we continued to try and figure out the other six faces of the mountain. We saved over 300 million dollars." With positive results like that, gaining the support of stakeholders was easy and helped lead the way for more improvements.

Figure 13.1 illustrates the seven faces up the mountain Interface has been following to scale the peak and achieve zero footprint.

Figure 13.1: Seven Fronts of Mount Sustainability Lead to Zero Footprint

Within the various fronts or faces of Mount Sustainability, Interface's model calls for :

1. Eliminating or reusing waste products
2. Eliminating the use of toxic products and hazardous chemicals
3. Operating facilities with 100 percent renewable energy
4. Redesigning products to close the technical loop using recovered or bio-based materials
5. Transport people and products efficiently to eliminate waste and emissions
6. Create a culture that uses sustainability principles to improve the lives of all stakeholders
7. Create a new business model that demonstrates and supports the value of sustainability-based commerce

In its drive to ascend Mount Sustainability Interface has worked to design lifecycle products, or products that can be recovered and turned into another useful product. In doing so the company has incorporated the methodology of biomimicry or using nature as a model for developing sustainable designs and processes.

A New Business Model

The change in the company's business model led to the development of "Evergreen Service Contracts." This means that Interface leases carpet services to customers rather than selling carpet that would end up as landfill. The company developed the concept of carpet tiles, which Interface maintains and selectively replaces. Like worn carpet, worn tiles are recycled and remanufactured into new products.

Yet another innovation of the Interface team is EcoMetrics, a set of measures that help assess the effect of changes. Specifically, EcoMetrics measure material and energy inputs and outputs, which in turn are used in benchmarking and to monitor environmental progress. According to its 2010 sustainability report, Interface has reduced its emissions significantly since 1996: greenhouse gas emissions are down by 44 percent in absolute terms, and by 94 percent when including offsets. Measuring outputs like these helps Interface set goals, and push toward becoming a restorative enterprise.

The company also aims for sustainable production by eliminating the use of hazardous chemicals and by tapping renewable energy sources to make facilities "green"—for instance, by installing skylights in factories to let in the warmth and light of the sun. Today, eight of Interface's nine manufacturing facilities operate with 100% renewable electricity. As is illustrated in figure 13.2, some 30 percent of the company's total energy usage in 2010 came from renewable energy sources.

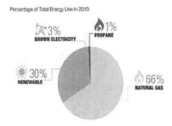

Figure 13.2: Interface's total energy use by source in 2010[167]

---

[167] Source: www.interface.com

Much like Leonardo DaVinci who studied birds to develop models of flight, Interface also follows the tenets of biomimicry—imitating the best ideas and designs in nature to answer questions and solve problems. For instance, Interface's carpets are designed not to show wear by mimicking patterns found in nature. The company also chooses not to use nonrenewable materials and instead relies heavily on sustainable options like organic wood, cotton, and hemp.

Meanwhile another way in which Interface pursues sustainability is by using the lifecycle assessment (LCA) technique to understand the effects of new materials and processes throughout the lifecycle of a product, from raw material extraction to product recycling. The company shares lifecycle assessment data with customers through its Environmental Product Declarations (EPDs), which provide unparalleled transparency on the effect of Interface's products on the environment. This step—the first in Interface's industry—goes above and beyond normal cooperation; it also sparks enthusiasm and energy among customers who like to know what the companies they patronize are doing for the environment.

Involving Employees to Change Company Culture

Internally, Interface values employee engagement through its QUEST program. "In nature there is no waste, so we set out on a quest, literally QUEST—Quality Using Employee Suggestions and Teamwork—to eliminate waste," said Anderson. QUEST, which has been in operation since 1995, challenges groups of 15 to 18 employees to identify every possible waste stream, to brainstorm feasible solutions, and to measure the savings and benefits of solutions implemented. Interface considers waste to be anything that does not add value for customers. The program, a hands-on alternative to the suggestion box, yields innovative thinking and gives employees a sense of ownership in the company's challenges and drive toward sustainability.

"We're changing minds and changing hearts, changing the culture of the company, changing the culture of the industry, and, in time, we might even change the culture of the culture. It's turning out to be a better way to make a bigger profit. The amazing thing is here we are eleven years into this journey and our costs have gone down not up. Our products are the best they have ever been, through David Oakey's adoption of biomimicry.... Today I would say that pioneering a new way of doing business is the ultimate purpose... that goes beyond the bottom line, a higher purpose, that all of us can subscribe to and be part of....”[168]

MEASURING SUSTAINABILITY AT INTERFACE

Employee Welfare. Interface takes care of its employees. The Interface culture is built on a belief that associates who are encouraged to take full advantage of their inherent strengths will be more satisfied, more engaged and more productive in their work. QUEST and the EcoSense training program help associates discover what sustainability means to Interface and how they can be a part of making it happen.

Financial. Interface is a billion dollar industrial carpet manufacturer and they have a high portion of the market. With their innovative carpet tiles they have established a competitive advantage. They save millions of dollars reducing waste and using renewable energy sources.

Supply Chain. Though one of their seven faces of Mount Sustainability is to encourage suppliers to be environmentally friendly, the information in this area is hard to find and the reduction in transportation costs is minimal.

Social. Interface has a strong positive connection with society. The company has changed its business model to develop a culture that incorporates sustainability with respect to all stakeholders.

Community. Interface employees are encouraged to volunteer and get involved in their local communities.

Environmental. This is where Interface scores the highest. They are consistently exceeding their previous years' goals of reducing waste and recycling. As their carpets are made from recycled carpet tiles they are persistently reducing waste. Employee's health is definitely high on the priority list. Interface is on its way to becoming a restorative enterprise and has been paving the way for other companies.

---

[168] Ray Anderson on Sustainability. www.youtube.com/watch?v=4bAdsJCHGyU

Results

Have the company's efforts paid off? You decide. Interface was listed among the Top Rated Companies for Sustainability 2010 in the Southeast by Green Business Works. Ray Anderson was recognized and rewarded in 2010 with the Lifetime Achievement Award at the Responsible Business Awards ceremony in London. And, with a strong following, Interface is leading the way to sustainability for large corporations. With its strong values and powerful mission, Interface is—and continues to strive to remain—a Good Company.

Cynthia Thi Nguyen provided research assistance in preparing this chapter.

CHAPTER 14
VESTAS WIND SYSTEMS

The Vestas of today—a global powerhouse with more than 20,000 employees worldwide—bears no resemblance to the one-man blacksmith shop that started it all. Originally founded in 1898 by H.S. Hansen in Denmark, the shop manufactured steel windows for industrial buildings. Work virtually stopped during World War II due to metal rationing, but after the war Hansen saw a need for household appliances and founded the company under the name VEstjyskSTålteknik A/S, understandably shortened to the name we know today: Vestas.[169]

The company's history for two decades thereafter tells a tale of serendipity. In 1950, Hansen fulfilled a desire to expand internationally by buying the worldwide patent for a milk urn cooler and by producing agricultural equipment, which he exported to Finland, Germany, and Belgium. In 1960, fire decimated Vestas' offices and warehouse, an unfortunate event that, fortunately, inspired a company "house cleaning" and filled staff with a strong desire to achieve more than ever before. Determined to overcome,

---

[169] http://www.vestas.com/en/about-vestas/profile/vestas-brief-history.aspx.

Vestas built a brand new factory and hired more workers, bringing the company headcount to 100 strong.

But it was the oil crisis of the 1970's that truly helped shaped Vestas into the company it is today. The crisis frustrated Vestas' leadership, inspiring them to consider alternative energy sources—including wind. Vestas soon began experimenting with wind turbine designs and was able to bring them to a hungry market by 1978. In 1986, the Danish government significantly cut the tax rebate on wind turbines, which slowed sales to a halt and pushed Vestas to the brink of bankruptcy. To slim down, leadership sold off much of the company, and a new firm with 60 employees emerged: Vestas Wind Systems A/S.

The new Vestas continued to profit and grow, going public in 1998 on the Copenhagen Stock Exchange. In 2004, the company merged with another Danish wind-turbine manufacturer, NEG Micon A/S. At the helm of the newly formed venture sat—and still sits—Ditlev Engel, President and CEO. Engel had previously served in various senior executive roles for the international Hempel Group, including Hempels Hong Kong, Norway, China, and, for his final post, Hempel Denmark.[170] Although the Hempel Group as a whole provides protective paint and coatings for numerous firms and products—including for Vestas' wind turbines[171]—Engle admits in his company-posted biography that he was not familiar with the company and its products when he came aboard in 1999.[172] That same biography describes how he served as heads of sales, marketing, and research and development, and how by May 2005, he had been installed as Group President and CEO of Vestas Wind Systems. Shortly after Engel became CEO, he published Vestas' 2005-2008 strategy, "The Will to Win," which projected a vision of the firm developing wind energy to the point where it is as practical as oil and gas energy.

---

[170] http://www.vestas.com/en/investor/corporate-governance/executive-management/ditlev-engel.aspx
[171] http://www.hempel.com/Internet/inecorporatec.nsf/vDOC/207FB384E7139219C1256BE4004DF139
?OpenDocument
[172] http://www.vestas.com/en/investor/corporate-governance/executive-management/ditlev-engel.aspx
http://www.vestas.com/Admin/Public/DWSDownload.aspx?File=%2fFiles%2fFiler%2fEN%2fInvestor
%2fCorporat e_governance%2fBio_DitlevEngel_UK.pdf

A Beneficial Business Model

Vestas is still pursuing the goal of preserving the environment today, following a new but similar strategy named "No. 1 in Modern Energy."[173] The firm continues to manufacture wind turbines and provides a suite of services that help companies plan for, install, and maintain its wind turbine products. Each part of each wind turbine - the blade, nacelle, tower, and control system - is manufactured in a different worldwide location and transported to a client's construction site unassembled.

But it is what happens post-manufacture and post-installation that differentiates Vestas in the wind turbine field: the company's turbine maintenance model is based on operational time rather than on down time, meaning that Vestas gets paid only when its turbines are functioning properly. If and when a turbine breaks down, it stops generating maintenance-contract revenue for the company. A maintenance agreement of this type paints a clear picture to clients and prospective clients that Vestas is committed to installing operational machinery. The agreement structure also helps Vestas maintain something of a perpetual operational scaffold on which leadership may nurture a culture of excellence.

A good example of Vestas' commitment to quality, and an example of a disaster-gone-right, is a large project at Horns Reef off of the western coast of Denmark. This 80-turbine project went terribly wrong when it became clear—just as Vestas finished installing the last turbine ahead of schedule—that every nacelle was defective. At a great loss, Vestas replaced each and every one of the 80 nacelles. While a major component failure is not the ideal way to illustrate reliability, it did, however, prove to clients current and future that Vestas does whatever it takes to get the job done.[174]

Interestingly, the reliability of Vestas' machinery provides another important benefit to potential clients—ease of financing. Banks are much more willing to finance a Vestas project because of the company's strong track record of reliability, as well as its proven ability to deliver low energy costs. Because the company consistently fulfills its promises of low-cost energy, it also delivers

---

[173] http://www.vestas.com/en/about-vestas/strategy.aspx.
[174] A nacelle is the housing for the blades that drive the turbine.

high business-case certainty, giving banks and clients the confidence they need that their wind turbine projects will achieve predicted financial returns.

Social and Environmental Mission

All for-profit companies, however, have a financial mission. What differentiates Vestas—indeed, what makes it a Good Company beyond its unique maintenance contract revenue model—are Vestas' social and environmental missions. Vestas implements its social mission through several partnerships and programs in China and in India.[175]Interestingly, Vestas partnered with Aravind Eye Systems, another company profiled in this book. In partnering with Aravind, Vestas helps fund rural eye-care clinics.[176] Other social programs in India include the "Little dreamers" program, which provides scholarships to rural youth who need help to complete schooling, and the "Carpentry Training Center," which uses wood packaging from the transportation of turbines as raw materials to train local youth in furniture building. The youth gain valuable experience working in a trade while providing furniture for schools—all from wood that would otherwise have been disposed.

Vestas, as a publicly traded company, seeks to achieve healthy financial returns, with a financial mission it calls "Triple 15." The goal is to achieve growth in revenues of €15 billion [US $20.5 billion] and profits of 15 percent by 2015. In 2010 revenues grew by 36 percent while profits rose by 6.8 percent , If the world economy improves, Vestas may be able to reach its goal of €15 billion in operating revenue by the year 2015.[177]

But where Vestas really shines is through its strong environmental mission, brought to life through both its "green" efforts and its manufacture of wind turbines, which is, by its very nature, an environmental mission. Vestas' self-proclaimed "as green as it gets" production method saves costs by reducing waste and secures the long-term availability of materials by focusing on sustainability. More important, its method is *marketable*. The company also

---

[175] http://www.vestas.com/en/media/news/news-display.aspx?action=3&NewsID=2390http://www.vestas.com/in/in/social-initiatives.aspx
[176] http://www.vestas.com/in/in/social-initiatives/key-projects/project-drishti.aspx
[177] www.vestas.com/en/media/news/news-display.aspx?action=3&NewsID=2563

employs a green building policy, a green car policy, and a green energy policy.[178]

Today, Vestas Wind Systems excels at keeping corporate sustainability at the core of its business, as well as at directly supporting the communities in which it operates and leading the market through a strong commitment to clients and quality.

Matt Fidge, MBA, assisted with the research for this chapter.

---

[178]http://workspace.imperial.ac.uk/careers/Public/AUDIO_VISUAL/forums/Energy%20Forum%20201 0/vestas_2704 10%20(2).pdf

CHAPTER 15

RECYCLA CHILE

Recycla Chile represents another company which has arisen in response to the range of environmental problems posed by electronic waste. Electronic waste is fast becoming a major issue around the world; e-waste is the fastest growing solid waste stream. In 2003 Fernando Nilo and Mauricio Nunez decided to do something about Chile's fast growing stream of e-waste. Chile, which is a small country of 17 million people and among the most prosperous countries of Latin America, is currently discarding 300,000 computers a year and at current trends will face a mountain of 1.7 million by 2020. Nilo and Nunez decided to start a company, the first in Chile and the first in Latin America that would employ the latest technology and methods for recycling.[179]

In 2004 they received funding from INOVA Chile, a national fund to promote entrepreneurship and innovation and provide support to start up businesses that generate a high economic and social impact. Partnering with OCTANTIS, a business incubator affiliated with the University of Adolfo Ibanez, to build a modern factory in the Santiago's industrial zone.

---

[179] Tyche Hendricks; "Second Chances and a Third Bottom Line." Stanford Social Innovation Review. Winter 2010. Pp 65-66

Octantis provided the advice and assisted with technology transfer taking a share much as a venture fund would do. But getting started was not easy Nilo says "It was very difficult, because here in Chile the environmental legislation and conscience is very weak."

The company's mission is "To collaborate with our clients in order to provide solutions to their electronic and industrial waste." Electronic waste can harbor lead, mercury, cadmium and other heavy metals. It is not uncommon for consumers and manufacturers to dump these e-wastes into landfills where they leach into groundwater and poison animals and people. Many countries export their e-waste only to find that is not a solution when the toxic materials in e-waste may end up as ingredients in products destined for consumer use such as jewelry imported from China.

And it is disastrous for the health of people who handle the waste improperly. "In Guiyu, China, for example, workers burn themselves with acid and clouds of burning plastic and lead fumes hover over an ash filled river." While in Ghana "children sift through mountains of shattered computers."[180] Each year over 400 million electronic devices end up in e-waste.[181]

Recycling Products –and People!

Nilo and Nunez looked at this social problem and saw an opportunity to develop a company to safely and ethically dismantle old computers and other e-waste while selling the valuable metal by-products. By 2010 the company was profitable and providing jobs for 25 people. The company even offered a second chance for people as well as products by employing ex-convicts and recovering drug addicts. Nilo adds "We're offering them a second chance in life. We're recycling them."

For example, Katherine Ortega released from prison for a drug trafficking offense was unable to find a job until she was connected with the company by a social worker. Her job, breaking and sorting computer components, has allowed her to rebuild her dignity.

---

[180] Hendricks pp 65-66.
[181] www.electronicstakeback.com/wp-content/uploads/Facts_and_Figures

Employees can count on receiving good salaries, stability and the opportunity for meaningful work. The company generates 'green jobs' for young professionals who seek good jobs which contribute to the community.

Recycla's Business Model

Recycla Chile's business model combines planet and profit. Chilean businesses pay the company to handle their e-waste with the company extracting and selling reusable materials—worth about $2 million annually and then paying an ISO certified hazardous waste processing center in Chile to dispose of the hazardous wastes. [182] The wastes are exported primarily to Europe since the company is wary of recycling practices in China and India and avoids sending its wastes to these countries even though it would be less costly and therefore more profitable.

Taking his business to the next level the company is incorporating education about e-waste into its mission. And Nilo is also working with Chile's Ministry of the Environment to encourage them to develop regulations and incentives such as requiring manufacturers to adopt 'cradle-to- grave' responsibility as a way to promote e-waste recycling.

As for the future, Nilo says "our dream is to recycle 10% of Chile's e-waste. Today we are recycling 2%. [But] to achieve this we will need support from different stakeholders, from government, NGOs, international funds and institutions among others." The challenge they face is "To introduce technology in our Recycling Plant, educate the companies and work towards having the same legislation as the European Union and USA."[183]

"The dream of RECYCLA is to support the building of a country which is in harmony with the environment as well as one with greater equality and innovative. We dream of replicating our vision in other countries around the world."

---

[182] www.electronicstakeback.com/wp-content/uploads/Facts_and_Figures
[183] http://www.idisc.net/en/Article.38520.html retrieved January 7, 2011.

CHAPTER 16
NATURA COSMETICOS

If you are planning for one year, plant grain. If you are planning for a decade, plant trees. If you are planning for a lifetime, enlighten the people."

KUAN CHUNG TSU

Long before most Brazilians were aware of climate change, in the early 1970s, natural products company Natura Cosmeticos set about creating a company where ecological concerns were more than skin deep. Today it is one of the best-known Brazilian brands for shampoos, cosmetics, creams and beauty products and a pioneer for sustainability.

In 1969, Cunha began Natura in a small corner store in Sao Paulo, Brazil where he kept daily contact with all his customers. He talked to them, listened to them, and began to understand the importance of dialogue in his approach to business and beauty.

Cunha met Guilherme Leal and Pedro Pasos in the 1970's, the three men formed a partnership and together built their philosophy of relationships that formed Natura, a cosmetics company with a strong brand and premium price and high profit margins, that is consistently rated as one of the best places to work in Brazil. The company's focus on social and environmental responsibility underpins its innovation. The company's emphasis on relationships bolstered by a shared love of beauty and strong employee motivation catapulted it to a leading role in Brazil's cosmetics, fragrances, and toiletries industry. [184]

In Brazil's fast-growing beauty products market, the fourth largest in the world, Natura competes against international heavyweights such as Avon, L'Oréal, Beiersdorf and Unilever. "Natura is well known in the market even among poorer sections of the society. 'The company is seen as ethical and can be trusted,' says Malak Poppovic, director of São Paulo-based human rights group Conectas. Although Natura faces fierce competition, the company believes that sustainability policies are more than just a marketing tool. Chief executive Alessandro Carlucci says that Natura is committed to its environmental initiatives for the long term, because they are good for business. "We did it because, for instance, we thought, 'Why should the customer pay for packaging if they can be refilled five times, which costs less for them and the environment?' "[185]

Luiz de Cunha, an economist with a dream to create beauty products, built his company around his values, seeing the world as an interconnected web of relationships. Natura's business model places emphasis on the importance of relationships.

Natura Cosméticos emerged as a cosmetics giant by dint of clever marketing and its firm commitment to sustainability. As The Economist noted the company, from its use of recyclable materials in its packaging to its advertising which uses ordinary women rather than supermodels, emphasizes naturalness and sustainability.

Starting with a direct sales (independent contractor/consultants) business model with an original team of 70 sales vendors, from its beginning Natura had a vision to become a leading manufacturer and marketer of skin care, cosmetics, perfume and hair care products in Brazil, with strong sales in Argentina, Columbia, Peru and Mexico.

Natura's motto is 'Bem estar bem': "Our Reason for Being is to create and sell products and services that promote well-being and being well. Well-being is the harmonious, pleasant relationship of a person with oneself,

---

[184] Robert G. Eccles, George Serafeim, James Heffernan   Source: Natura Cosmeticos S.A. Harvard Business School. 2006
[185] http://www.ethicalcorp.com/content.asp?ContentID=6076&rss=ec-main.xml

with one's body. Being well is the empathetic, successful, and gratifying relationship of a person with others, with nature and with the whole."[186]

Natura's manufacturing and business headquarters are located in a beautiful and environmentally protected area outside of Sao Paulo. They have production facilities in two locations in Brazil, and they have distribution centers in all of their main international locations.

The company produces a variety of cosmetics, fragrances, and personal hygiene products with a product portfolio that consists of approximately 900 products investing heavily in R&D. By striving for continuous improvement and innovation the company introduced 191 new products in 2010.

Natura's Business Model

Natura uses direct sales through a network of independent consultants who constitute its sales force. The company has consistently increased the size of its sales force, from the original 70 sales consultants to over 1.2 million sales consultants in 2010. Because the company philosophy is based around the idea of nurturing relationships, this naturally extends to their sales force as well. They realize that their sales force is the face of their company, and therefore they must reflect the company's belief in the importance of relationships to everyone they come into contact with. The combination of quality products and good marketing has proven to be an explosive mixture for the direct selling method, helping to make the company extremely profitable.

Natura provides training for their sales associates through frequent workshops and acknowledge consultants through recognition programs for company longevity, sales volume and number of customers. Managers stay connected to their sales force, and learn from their various experiences and

---

[186] www2.natura.com.br The tagline is a pun. The literal translation from Portuguese into English would be "well-being/being well". It means that Natura strives, through its products and services, to help people enjoy better relationships with themselves (well-being), with others, with nature and the world around them (being well)." Source
http://www.food.wi.tum.de/index.php?id=14&L=1&tx_ttnews%5Btt_news%5D=36&cHash=fb7de5ef8
caea4bf5e1fe23e0a3367cf

insights through a company intranet system, set up to share ideas and give feedback. These various efforts have helped keep employee satisfaction high and turnover low.

Research and development also plays a big role in the company's success. "Natura is ... a master of what might be dubbed "lean innovation", noted The Economist. "About 40 percent of its revenues come from products introduced in the past two years. But the company has only about 150 research and development staff compared with L'Oréal's 2,800. Its trick is to form partnerships with foreign universities and to scour the world for products that it can license."[187]

A Sustainable Strategy

Natura is a mission driven company with sustainability at the core of the company's $2.5 billion operation.

Natura currently has operations in 44 different countries, with distribution centers in Argentina, Chile, Peru, Columbia, Mexico and France. The company strategy is to be able to move in, get along, and become part of the new market and community. They promote diversity, and this includes respecting the diversity of other cultures. Production is in Brazil at its two production centers, although there are plans for production centers in Argentina and Columbia. In Argentina and Peru they are now among the top three preferred brands. Looking towards the future of their international involvement the company is working to gain increased regionalized product portfolios and promotions, localized promotions, greater knowledge on the consumption habits of local consumers, and familiarizing with regional opportunities.

Natura is committed to nurturing these international relationships, working for local causes, and working to overcome social and environmental challenges in each unique area they are involved in. They will continue to increase their commitment to local causes and social and environmental challenges.

---

[187] The Economist. Brazilian model: Brazil needs to be more innovative to fulfill its promise of being the "country of the future" Nov 18 2010

Ethical Sourcing

In order to ensure that ingredients derived from Brazilian flora are harvested using socially and environmentally sound practices, Natura designed its Program for Certification of Suppliers of Forest Products striving to protect the Brazilian biodiversity, and taking care to use sustainable practices for the extraction of these raw materials. They have agreements with 19 different traditional communities (small villages in the Amazon), both to source products, as well as gain local knowledge on these items that have been used in traditional practices for generations from the people that know them best. Their agreements are based on sharing benefits, image use rights, and local sustainable development plans. Each agreement is carried out by a multidisciplinary team that assesses every relationship based on benefit sharing, mobilization for economic sustainability, relationship channels, and satisfaction with the commercial relationship.

Brazil's rich biodiversity, with millions of people living from the land has encouraged Natura to help educate them on diversifying the products they farm, and work with them to come up with new ideas on how to utilize their products. Benefits provided by Natura include a focus on technology transfer, capacity building, improved livelihood, skills and education, as well as support for local conservation efforts. Indigenous communities have benefited by gaining new skills, a greater understanding of sustainable economic activities relating to bio-diverse genetic resources, and are participating in new economic relationships with Natura that contribute to greater economic stability in their communities.

Social and Environmental Mission

The company is committed to the shared value model demonstrating this with the creation of a program to improve public education in Brazil and other countries in which they operate. They also contribute to the Trilhas project (with more than 200,000 students), helping to fight against illiteracy.

Natura's focus is on the use of natural ingredients, including essences and oils of everything from avocado to passion fruits. It was the first Brazilian company to use refillable containers, and committed itself to reduce its greenhouse gas emissions by 33% before 2011. It phased out animal testing, along with all petroleum and animal based ingredients. Among the environmental goals are lowering their carbon emissions as well as their water usage.

Natura aligned their 2010 targets with their socio-environmental budget to further integrate sustainability with the strategic planning cycle. At the headquarters a water treatment facility takes in water from the Jaqueri river, uses the water for operations where it is treated and re-used and recycled four different times before it flows back into the river, cleaner than when it came in.

The company operates its entire distribution fleet on natural gas while also seeking to limit the amount of plastic packaging it uses. Petrochemicals will continue to have a role, but their use is constantly decreasing. For example, Natura's Ekos line of shampoos uses 30 percent recycled ingredients.

CEO Alessandro Carlucci, who has headed the company since 2005, warns that sometimes this ecological brand reputation can raise expectations higher than the company can deliver. Despite this João Meirelles, director general of environmental non-governmental organization Instituto Peabiru, says although Natura tries to do the right thing, "Sometimes they source materials from a handful of suppliers, while they should really try to extend this to a wider community." In general Meirelles is encouraged by Natura's approach. He says: "They are open to critical ideas and accept them, which is positive and rare in business."[188]

Natura's mission and its corporate culture have been based on respect for the environment, social responsibility, and a concern for passing on a healthier planet to future generations. Sustainable development is a way of managing the earth's resources so that those living today, as well as those who come later, will have continued access to those resources. One of their founding principles was sustainability, which served as a guide for their business for over 40 years.

The company has received numerous awards for their environmental and social efforts including Most Sustainable Company in South America, the

---

[188] http://www.ethicalcorp.com/content.asp?ContentID=6076&rss=ec-main.xml

Brazil Environmental Award, The 100 Best in Corporate, Civic Responsibility 2008, Corporate Civic Responsibility award from AMCHAM Argentina.

Financial Results

The company reported $401 million in net income on $2.5 billion in net revenues for 2010, demonstrating that you don't have to give up your ideals or vision to be profitable.

Shennon O'Donnel provided research assistance in preparing this chapter.

CHAPTER 17

SMA SOLAR TECHNOLOGIES

Shortly after completing their engineering degrees in 1981, Gunther Cramer and Peter Drews realized that photovoltaic markets was poised to become increasingly important and decided to stake their careers on renewable energy. They set a goal to commercialize the emerging solar technology industry of the late 20th century. Today SMA Solar Technology is the largest manufacturer of power inverters, essential components of solar panels that transform sunlight into electricity.

The company's mission is to "make the installation and operation of photovoltaic power plants even simpler, more reliable, safer, and above all, more cost effective."[189] Inverters are a crucial part of any solar system; they convert the power which comes from solar panels in direct current (DC) to alternating current (AC), the type of power used in homes and businesses. Their versatile products are compatible with any source of energy including hydroelectric, wind, and bio/gas generators.

SMA's key strategy from the very beginning was to emphasize cutting edge technology.

---

[189] www.sma-america.com

The company's inverters operate at over 98% efficiency; no other products on the market are able to operate at this level, giving SMA Solar Technology a competitive advantage.[190] In addition to their inverters, they also offer solar design services, on-site services for their products, wind power DC to AC inverters, software, fuel cell inverters and monitoring systems. An example of a system they've designed is the Sunny Island, an off-grid electricity supply in remote locations, such as villages in developing nations.

SMA Solar Technology also offers training services for owners and users of their products. Located at the SMA Solar Academy, they help soon-to-be customers pick which SMA systems will be best for them, and help develop communication methods and channels regarding photovoltaic systems.

Their products are used on every continent, including the Princess Elisabeth Station in Antarctica. Cramer noted "SMA as a technology and global market leader with 17 foreign subsidiaries situated on four continents is exceptionally well prepared for the further internationalization of our business. Our extreme flexibility and the consistent expansion of our production capacities means that we are perfectly prepared for weathering the high volatility of the solar markets." [191]

Producing products in the markets that they are sold gives SMA Solar Technology a few strategic advantages.[192] First, they're able to secure high levels of market share, making it tough for competitors to break in once SMA Solar Technology is established. By working closely with their local customers, SMA customizes the products for the local market. For example, power inverters sold in the US are manufactured to a certain size so that they can adhere to US construction codes.

---

[190] http://www.sma.de also see "SMA - the biggest producer of solar energy inverters." - Accessed on 4/30/11 http://www.youtube.com/watch?v=KZQ_TjZkoyA

[191] SMA Solar Technology's export ratio has more than doubled over the last five years, increasing from 20.1% in 2006 to nearly 45% in 2010. According to their 2010 Annual Report, "Two thirds of the photovoltaic markets were already outside Germany in 2010. This is also the reason why we increasingly see the need to locally produce in some markets – directly for the corresponding market in that country." SMA Solar Technology 2010 Annual Report, English Version.

[192] www.sma.de

Taking Care of Its People

Having previously worked in a corporate setting, the founders decided that SMA's corporate culture was to be special; employee participation in decision-making is a central element. "We encourage our employees to act independently and with great commitment, to contribute their knowledge and assist in a constructive manner in shaping the company's development." The keys to this are: open communication on all levels, involvement in setting company goals, opportunities for further training and a profit sharing program.

In an industry dominated by male employees, women currently make up 25 percent of their workforce and 15 percent of their managers. In mid-2011, SMA Solar Technology started an initiative to increase those numbers. In 2011, SMA received the first place award for "Great Place to Work" in a German competition for companies with more than 5,000 employees.[193]

An Environmental Innovator

The very nature of the solar industry is expanding the use of clean, renewable energies. However, their corporate culture pushes the company beyond this. Their main production facility based in Germany is CO_2 neutral. This facility was opened in 2009 and is the location of final assembly for most of their products. As one might expect, the SMA Solar Academy is energy self-sufficient and carbon neutral and is powered from solar panels on the building, and in tracking-arrays located around the building. Photovoltaic units are helping to power a large portion of other buildings owned by SMA Solar Technology, and include charging stations for electric vehicles.

In addition to their production facilities, their production processes are also geared toward improving the quality of materials and the efficiency of the products themselves, since improved efficiency of the inverters results in improved efficiency in power generation from photovoltaic sources.

As a result SMA was admitted to the German Partnership for Climate Protection and Energy Efficiency in October 2010. And in 2011 it received

---

[193] www.sma.de

environmental management certification, ISO 14001, from the International Standards Office in Switzerland.

Benefiting the Community

Beyond this, SMA Solar Technology has created a product that is specifically designed to serve remote villages in emerging economies. The Sunny Island system is an off-grid photovoltaic system, designed to be compatible with any type of power source, including hydroelectric, wind energy, and bio/gas generators. SMA Solar Technology partnered with the Institute of the University of Kassel and the German Ministry of Economics to bring this system to many locations, including villages in China, Thailand, Nepal, India, United Arab Emirates, Uganda, South Africa, Kenya, Greece, and Brazil. According to Chief Product Officer Peter Drews, with adequate funding, this type of system could bring electricity to 1 billion people around the world by 2015.[194]

SMA Solar Technology holds its suppliers to strict standards by requiring suppliers to sign the inter-branch Code of Conduct issued by the German Association Materials Management, Purchasing and Logistics. In addition to this, SMA has developed its own guidelines for suppliers using the company's values and international standards. They take care to monitor their suppliers to ensure adherence to the framework. The company's policies describe SMA's expectations for its suppliers and business partners by specifying fair working conditions and setting standards for product quality and safety.[195]

Financial Results

SMA Solar Technology demonstrates that the connection between its values—treating employees fairly, respecting the environment and contributing to the community have produced a superior technology resulting in sales of $2.8 billion and profits of $541 million in 2010.[196]

Stephen Kirschenmann and Mireya Ruiz provided research assistance.

---

[194] "Sunny Island - The Ruler of the Solar Kingdom" – Accessed on 4/30/11
http://www.youtube.com/watch?v=d09_3lBxyn4

[195] Findings are reported in the 2010 Annual Voluntary Disclosure.

[196] www.Businessweek.com and www.SMA.de/IR/FinancialReports

CHAPTER 18

EILEEN FISHER

When Eileen Fisher founded her company in 1984, she had just $350 in the bank and a vision of making clothing with simple shapes from good fabric. When a friend suggested she take over his booth at a New York Designs show, she emerged with $3000 in orders. Three months later, she had sold $40,000 and took the stack of orders to a bank to borrow the money to make them. "They laughed, 'How do we know that these orders are real orders? Or that these stores are credit-worthy?' I had no idea. So I borrowed money from friends and did the order in shifts."[197]

"If I had really known what it meant to start a business, I probably would have been too scared to go ahead," she recalled in a 1994 *Forbes* article.

Eileen Fisher was now in business. "I put the pieces together one day at a time, one step at a time," she later told Donna Fenn for *Executive Female*. "I still find that's an important way to do things." The company doubled its first $50,000 in annual revenue during the second year and again in the third.

---

[197] Eileen Fisher. Inc. Magazine www.inc.com/hidi

Revenues reached $1.3 million in 1988, the year she married David Zwiebel, owner of a New York boutique who stocked her garments. He became vice-president, convinced her to open her own stores, and by 1991 the company had earned over $7 million in annual sales. Applying its simple styles and way of doing business, sales grew to $25 million by 1993.

But the rapid expansion resulted in an all too common setback. As a result of time pressure, Fisher ordered $1 million worth of wool tweed before it made a sample. The fabric didn't work well and the garments didn't sell, so she had to sell about 20 percent of the line at a loss. "Chastened, [she] brought in key buyers early the next season to show them samples and get their opinions on what would sell. She also sent a staff member to the factory for preproduction sampling in order to reduce approval time on fabric quality."[198]

By 1995 sales reached $50 million, sourcing about 40 percent of sales out of China and Hong Kong. The company also opened boutiques in department stores in Tokyo. By 2010 Eileen Fisher annual sales had reached about $250 million.

Secret of Success: Taking Care of People

If you ask Amy Hall, Eileen Fisher's Director of Social Consciousness, the secret to the company's success, the answer is simple: "If you get the people and the product right, the rest will follow. We spend lots of time listening to our employees and our customers. That's our culture—to talk directly with all of our stakeholders and engage with them. People love working here; we are regularly rated among the top ten places to work."[199]

Eileen Fisher's first priority was to create a great place to work. "As a woman she recognized that we all have lives and that entails other responsibilities," says Hall. "All of this reflects our mission: to nourish well-being in mind, body, and spirit and to infuse positive energy into our everyday experience."

Why is that? Hall says "Everything at Eileen Fisher is highly collaborative, open, and interactive. We have a highly unusual leadership model. Eileen

---

[198] http://www.fundinguniverse.com/company-histories/Eileen-Fisher-Inc-Company-History.html
[199] Personal interview November 2008.

delegates completely, and that's why she sold the company back to the employees. She wanted to maintain our culture and keep the company from being acquired by anyone who would not respect our culture."[200]

Fisher regards the employee's whole life as the company's responsibility. To achieve this, the company incorporates a variety of benefits into its culture such as its comprehensive wellness program that includes $100 annual reimbursement for education, yoga, and exercise. Each week the company brings to its site specialists in yoga therapy and reflexology as well as other health practitioners who put on free workshops. The company has flexible working hours and an on-site lactation room. In addition, it offers three months of paternity leave. Fisher believes that profits flow from treating one's employees with dignity and respect.

When Fisher decided to move the company to the suburbs, she selected a site convenient to public transportation and paid employees' commuting expenses. Moreover, employees received profit sharing equal to ten percent of the firm's profits at year-end.

Collaborative Leadership

Leadership plays an enormous role at Eileen Fisher. The company is managed by a 20-person forum consisting of departmental and area leaders. Three facilitating leaders are in charge of keeping the leadership team on track in all its meetings and deliberations. The company prides itself on encouraging employees to stretch and build their skills. Equally important are opportunities to let employees follow their passions.

To illustrate, the company's unique fashion designs emerge from a process called a "Deep Dive, in which about 80 to 100 employees from all parts of the company, including pattern cutting, sales, design, and retail get together for two days to discuss ideas. Creativity is fostered through meditation and movement and conversations with customers. Jim Gundell, Vice President of Retail and E-commerce, says "Here I feel all psyched, because we know that we become more creative together. It's an incredible high."[201]

---

[200] Personal interview November 2008.
[201] More Magazine. May 2008. Pp. 86-88.

Fisher makes profits through its wide range of products that flatter most body types while being sustainable and fashionable. Eileen Fisher follows no trends; but rather makes comfortable and classic products that transcend fashion trends. Because of its commitment to quality and its social responsibility, the company can sell its products at a premium; garments typically range from $100 to $400.

Social Consciousness: Benefiting the Community

"So many of us have been able to find a place in Eileen Fisher that allows us to express our own interests and pursue what we feel passionately about," says Hall. "I started 15 years ago as assistant to the CEO, which was when we had a CEO instead of our current leadership team. I came from a career in nonprofit fundraising; I have a strong need to give back to society. When I came here, I was able to handle all of our donations since no one else had the interest or experience. As the company grew, so did our donations and so did my job. About three years ago I became the director of social consciousness, creating my own job around my passion to serve others."[202]

The company's annual Social Consciousness Report points to four areas: employee wellness, community support, protection of the environment, and human rights. The employee/owners feel these are essential to achieving their vision.[203] The social consciousness team seeks answers to three key questions:

- How can we do our work in a socially conscious way?
- How can we further embed socially conscious values throughout the company?
- How can we influence change beyond our company walls?[204]

---

[202] Personal interview November 2008.

[203] Because only 10 to 15 percent of the clothing it sells comes from the United States while 80 percent is sourced from China and the remainder comes from India, Peru, and Portugal, Eileen Fisher must pay close attention to its global supply chain. The company has met this challenge for the past ten years by partnering with compliance firms like InterTech, which handles its relations with suppliers in China.

[204] Amy Hall. "Engaging Employees in Social Consciousness at EILEEN FISHER;" Journal of Organizational Excellence. Autumn 2006. Pp. 45-52.

Through its grant-making program and a variety of store events, Eileen Fisher commits five percent of each year's profits to support socially responsible organizations and groups working domestically and internationally.[205]

Supporting women through social initiatives that address their well-being is another aspect of Fisher's vision achieved by guiding product and processes towards sustaining the environment and by practicing business responsibly with absolute regard for human rights. Eileen Fisher continually seeks new and innovative ways to empower women around the globe to find their voices and achieve emotional, spiritual, and physical well-being. It is its hope to become more proactive in this effort, seeking out nonprofit organizations and causes that best encompass its philanthropic mission and supports issues women feel passionate about.

The company's philosophy of supporting the community and its commitment to the well-being of its staff, customers, and the larger community emanates directly from Eileen Fisher's desire to help women achieve simplicity and balance in their lives. The company supports programs that advance women's and girl's self-image.

The Eileen Fisher Business Grant Program for Woman Entrepreneurs was launched in 2004 with a single grant to commemorate the company's 20th anniversary. Since then, five grants have been awarded each year. The program seeks applicants from wholly women-owned businesses that combine the principles of social consciousness, sustainability, and innovation to create new businesses or invigorate existing ones. For example, one beneficiary was To-Go Ware, based in Berkeley, California. To-Go Ware makes durable, reusable utensils out of environmentally responsible materials and incorporates fair trade practices into its production.

The company provides grants to assist women entrepreneurs with a strong vision and a solid business plan. In addition, through a matching gift program, it matches up to $1,000 per employee and donates $100 to any charity for which an employee is raising funds through a walk, run, or

---

[205] www.eileenfisher.com

similar event. A donations committee, made up of representatives from across the company, holds regular meetings to review and decide on all requests for support of social initiatives that address the well-being of women. Among the causes the company has supported are a health center to help low-income Latina women afflicted by chronic pain and alternative health care for low-income women suffering from cancer.

Respecting Human Rights

Eileen Fisher manufactures 90 percent of its products overseas, with 80 percent coming from China and the remainder from India, Peru, and Portugal, so human rights are an issue. The company does not own any factories; most of the factories it works with produce other major brands as well. Beginning in 1998, the company created the position of leader of social consciousness in order to address human rights issues in the factories of its suppliers, including ten plants in China.

The company sees its manufacture of clothing as an opportunity to improve the working conditions and facilitate change in its partner factories. The company employs Verite, an audit firm, to help monitor its overseas factories; workers receive monthly interactive education on topics such as workplace safety, labor rights, and women's health.

Using SA8000, an internationally recognized workplace standard based on UN and International Labor Organization conventions, the company is committed to promoting fundamental human rights in nine areas, including no child or forced labor, respect for freedom of association, reasonable working hours, protection of worker health, and safety. The company partners with social compliance audit firms to visit the factories, monitor conditions, and train factory managers to improve their methods or communication, and to respect factory workers.

Environmental Stewardship

At Eileen Fisher, sustainability efforts are separated into four boxes of activities. The first box focuses on sustainable design where the company pays attention to sustainability incorporated into the design of clothing and materials used; the amount of recycled paper content and sustainable inks used for brochures; and sustainability applied to the design of the company's buildings and infrastructure. The Architecture Design Department recommends eco-smart materials and designs such as the use of solar tint on windows to increase heating and cooling efficiency in new buildings and renovated office spaces. The second box pertains to recycling and reuse of materials and byproducts in the company's activities. The retail staff works to reduce the amount of plastic and paper waste generated by its stores promoting reuse of paper bags, boxes, and plastic hangers. The third box takes the second box a step further and evaluates the company's connection to its suppliers and efforts to engage them in environmental sustainability. The final box looks at the organization's impact on climate change including the company's measurement of its carbon footprint and an in-house 'eco-audit' intended to help identify opportunities to make progress toward more sustainable practices.

The company has built its products around the notion of sustainability. "By using organic rather than conventionally produced cotton, we are considering the cotton farmers and their communities; the workers who spin the fabric; the workers who manufacture the garment; our employees who handle and sell the pieces; and, ultimately our customer."[206]

Success Follows Values

The company has received a number of awards including Great Place to Work Institute, 25 Best Medium Companies to Work for in America, and Nordstrom's Partners in Excellence Award.

Eileen Fisher's revenues are poised to reach about $300 million in 2011. Although successful, Fisher says, "I don't think about my business so much in quarters of numbers that way. I think about getting the product right. If you do, the money will follow."[207]

---

[206] www.eileenfisher.com
[207] Eileen Fisher. Inc. Magazine www.inc.com/hidi

CHAPTER 19

GOOGLE

"Google is not a conventional company. We do not intend to become one."[208]

If any company is emblematic of success in the 21st century, it's Google, known the world over as the leader in connecting people with information. Google began with a grand vision: to organize the world's information and make it universally accessible and useful. In just over a decade, Google has made itself a global brand bigger than GE, McDonalds, or Disney.[209] Just five years after its birth as a company, the company's name literally became a verb, "google." Google leads the internet information industry with revenues totaling $29 billion and profits of $8.5 billion generated from its search engine, advertising, computer hardware, e-mail, android phone, and Internet services.[210]

Not only is Google among the world's largest companies, it has also ranked in the top ten of Fortune's "50 Most Admired Companies" and "Best Companies to Work For" lists every year since 2007.[211] As noted technology writer James Gleick writing in an August 2011 issue of the New York Review, said,

---

[208] Google IPO 2004. Quoted in Ken Auletta Googled. Penguin. 2009 p.289

[209] Source: http://interbrand.com/en/best-global-brands/best-global-brands-2008/best-global-brands-2010.aspx retrieved Sept 12, 2011

[210] Google 2010 10K Report; http://finance.yahoo.com/q/ae?s=GOOG+Analyst+Estimates

[211] Fortune Magazine. Fortune 500

"[Google] has created more wealth faster than any company in history; it dominates the information economy."[212] But it hasn't always been so.

A Brief History

Larry Page and Sergey Brin met at Stanford University; Brin was on the orientation team that welcomed Page to his computer engineering studies in 1995. Both were standouts in Stanford's engineering school for their boldness and dedication to building an efficient search engine that would supplement the limited human brain. One night while sleeping, Page bolted upright from a dream with a sudden vision. "I was thinking: What if we could download the whole Web and just keep the links.... I grabbed a pen and started writing." He shared his vision with Brin and the two set to work creating a search engine they first called BackRub.[213]

Page and Brin renamed the search engine Google, a word play on 'googol,' a mathematical term for the number represented by the numeral 1 followed by 100 zeros and a metaphor for the seemingly infinite amount of information available on the World Wide Web. Page and Brin opened Google's first office in the living room of their Escondido Village duplex. Ram Shriram, a well-connected angel investor realized that the two had developed a unique technology; he, along with three others, put in $1 million to help the visionaries get started in a dreary office in Menlo Park. In 1998, PC Magazine recognized the superiority of Google's search engine.[214] Then in June 1999, Omid Kurdistan negotiated a deal to designate Google as the default search engine for the then popular Netscape browser.[215]

The key to Google's success was its PageRank search engine. Before Google, most Internet searches yielded endless lists of disorganized 'hits' that users had to spend hours plundering trying to find one or two that might be of value. Google's PageRank algorithm uses the Web's implicit knowledge to

---

[212] James Gleick. "How Google Dominates us." New York Review. Aug 18, 2011 p 24
[213] Ken Auletta. Googled. p.35.
[214] December 1998 "PC Magazine reports that Google 'has an uncanny knack for returning extremely relevant results' and recognizes us as the search engine of choice in the Top 100 Web Sites for 1998"
[215] Ken Auletta. Googled. Penguin 2009. p. 56

rank order search results based on how many other pages are linked to a page. Before Google, websites and search engines maximized stickiness— the ability to prolong the user's stay on the site—over efficiency. Google changed all of that.[216]

Page and Brin's vision was that Google would be a sort of 'digital Switzerland,' a neutral search engine that favored no particular content or advertiser but would rely instead on the wisdom of the crowd. Google's technology copies the entire web, storing web pages on hundreds and thousands of personal computers that work in tandem. Past searches, meanwhile, are stored on servers so that Google doesn't have to search the web each time that a particular search is requested.[217] Google outpaced all of its rivals because the items at the top of a search are those most relevant to the user. The company's proprietary PageRank model favors web links that generate the most traffic and come from reliable sources such as The New York Times.

As a result, the company grew rapidly, adding clients worldwide. In 2000, Google offered searches in 15 different languages on google.com. In 2001, Eric Schmidt, a seasoned computer industry professional from Sun Microsystems and Novell joined Page and Brin. By 2002, Google had indexed 3.1 billion web pages, or about 80 percent of the World Wide Web. Its language offerings had grown to 72 as the company added major partnerships with AOL using CompuServe, Netscape and AOL.com. By 2004, Google, a babe at only five years old, was still a privately held company handling 85 percent of Internet searches and worth $25 billion. In 2005, the company hit a new milestone: 6 billion items, including 4.28 billion web pages and 880 million images.[218] And by 2009, the company

---

[216] Steven Levy. In the Plex: How Google Thinks, Works and Shapes our Lives. Simon and Schuster. 2011.

[217] Ken Auletta Googled p. 6.

[218] Over the next two years Google grew by acquisitions of Keyhole (the basis for Google Earth), Urchin (the basis for Google Analytics), dMarc (digital radio advertising), Writely (the basis for Google Docs) and YouTube and added offices in Ireland, Tokyo, and Mexico. Then the company added Google Maps, GoogleTalk, Mobile Web Search, Personalized Search, Blog Search, and Google Analytics, Chat in Gmail, Google News for mobile, Google Calendar, Google Trends, Google Checkout, Patent Search and continued its acquisitions and Jotspot (which becomes Google Sites). Google Voice, Google Latitude, Ventures, Toolbar labs, All for Good, Google buzz, Google Instant, Government Request Tools, Google TV, Caffeine.

had scanned or indexed over 25 billion web pages and recorded over three million searches per day.

Google's Business Model

Advertising drives Google's business model. Any and every market that attracts advertising is a potential money maker. Google earns its revenue by shaping its technology to maximize advertising revenues using performance-based advertising. According to Gleick, "More than 96 percent of [Google's] $29 billion in revenue came directly from advertising and most of the rest came from advertising related services."[219]The remaining revenues came from licensing its search engine, Internet mobile services, and online video.

Randall Stross, in his book Planet Google, observed that Google had neither expected nor wanted to leverage an advertising-based revenue model.

"Google's dependence on text ads is especially remarkable given that advertising was entirely absent in the original biasness plans of the founders. When the Google search engine was first made available to the public, visitors noticed superior search results, but they also noticed the service was entirely free of commercial messages.... Brin and Page were hostile to the very notion of permitting advertising on a search site."[220]

The company's search engine allowed Google to achieve a superior match between user and advertiser. With the company's modification of its AdWords advertising platform in 2002, it shifted from charging advertisers on a cost per thousand views (CPM) to a cost per click (CPC). This novel approach opened online advertising to millions of small businesses, thus democratizing advertising.

Google augmented its AdWords CPC model in 2003 with the addition of AdSense, which added sponsored ads to online searches. As Ken Auletta, in his book Googled, explained, "People looking at a web site devoted to

[219] James Gleick. "How Google Dominates us." New York Review. Aug 18, 2011 p 25
[220] Randall Stross. Planet Google. Free Press 2008. P 3. In 2000 some 85 percent of all searches showed no advertisements.

pancreatic cancer could see ads devoted to pharmaceuticals, Google would serve as the matchmaker, delivering the advertising and sharing the revenues."[221] AdSense essentially turned each person's search into a billboard for Google ads. As Google's current senior vice president of advertising explained in Auletta's book, the new model "...changed the way content providers think about business. They know they can generate revenues without having their own sales team."[222] Later, with the addition of Google Analytics, advertisers could also track the day-by-day, hour-by-hour, effectiveness of their ads by measuring the number of views that became purchases.

AdWords and AdSense became the juice of growth for Google's business.[223] "For the first time, in 2001, Google turned a profit: $7 million on revenues of $86 million. The next year, revenues more than quadrupled to $439 million, and profits jumped to $100 million."[224]

Such an exponential increase came primarily because Google could grow quickly at a low cost and multiply its revenue alongside the size of its user base. As Siva Vaidhyanathan noted in his book The Googleization of Everything, "We are not Google's customers: we are its product. We—our fancies, fetishes, predilections and preferences—are what Google sells to advertisers." By 2008, Google had transformed itself from a technology company to a software, technology, Internet, advertising, and media company all in one.

---

[221] Ken Auletta. Googled p. 91

[222] Susan Wojcicki quoted in Ken Auletta Googled p. 92

[223] Along with its ongoing evolution in revenue models, Google's business model evolved over the last decade from sponsored links to artificial intelligence driven targeted marketing. After its start up in 2000 the company sold "premium sponsored links" or text advertisements attached to search terms. Advertisers paid according to how many people viewed their ad. The next stage came after Google acquired GoTo start-up and Google changed from charge per view to charge per click. They also added another feature letting advertisers bid for key words in a fast on-line auction. All the while Google was monitoring user behavior and observing which ads were successful. More effective ads were given better placement earning the company and the advertiser more revenue and changing the old approach to advertising. The current evolution of the business model is called AdSense and uses artificial intelligence to predict what type of advertisement would appeal to a particular user. This widely expanded the number of advertisers and possible placements "because the ads were so powerfully, measurably productive.' Ads might appear in your Gmail as a result of something that you mentioned in a message.

[224] Ken Auletta. Googled p. 92

With its superior ability to analyze and use vast amounts of data, Google attracts large numbers of users and then connects those users to products they might wish to buy. Google's open content approach, in contrast to the closed strategy of competitors like Microsoft and Yahoo, also attracts a larger audience of users. And this feeds into a fourth key element, co-creation, in which Google gives a variety of independent actors the tools they need to create new services, thus enabling Google to reach new markets.

The company has worked to build large-scale solutions to a wide range of issues. As Eric Schmidt explained at a public forum, "We often do things that don't make any sense from traditional norms. And we're proud of that, and we talk about that. The founders have set the mission of the company—that we work on big problems that affect people at scale that have not been solved before."[225]

Today, Google keeps its brands strong by branching out to other areas, acquiring pertinent companies, and continuing to diversify on multiple fronts. Its business strategy calls for operating in every Internet area, distinguishing products with superior design, building awareness, and making products widely and easily accessible. Google also continually updates its products by adding features regularly.

Today's Google is able to price its products above average because of its superior performance. The company also partners with rivals such as Yahoo and AOL to increase its ability to gather data on customers and better tailor its business products to meet customer demands. For example, in 2000, the company offered Google Earth in 10 language versions; by 2002, Google had added another 62 language interfaces, including the fictional language familiar to Star Trek lovers everywhere—Klingon.

---

[225] Randall Stross. Planet Google. Free Press 2008. P 15

A People Culture

Beyond its impressive technology capabilities and revenue model, Google is perhaps best known for being a great place to work. Its headquarters in Mountain View, California, comprises a collection of interconnected low-rise buildings that look more like a college campus than a corporate office complex. Employees get free meals three times a day; free use of an outdoor wave pool, an indoor gym, and a large childcare facility; private shuttle bus service to and from San Francisco and other residential areas; and free onsite medical care and subsidized massages. Employees are also encouraged to propose and test wild, ambitious ideas to see if they work.

A stroll through the Google campus reveals further signs of Google's people-first culture:

- Bicycles or scooters for efficient travel between meetings
- Dogs, lava lamps, massage chairs, and large inflatable balls
- Googlers sharing cubes, yurts and huddle rooms—and very few solo offices
- Laptops everywhere—laptops being standard issue for mobile coding, email, and on-the- go note-taking
- Foosball and pool tables, volleyball courts, assorted video games, pianos, Ping-Pong tables, and gyms that offer yoga and dance classes
- Break rooms packed with a variety of snacks and drinks to keep Googlers going
- Healthy lunches and dinners for all staff at a variety of cafés

When its creative culture led to a 2010 increase in revenue by more than 20 percent, Google responded by giving each employee a 10-percent pay hike. Employees can also receive $175 peer spot-bonuses, awarded by their fellow employees; in 2010, more than two thirds of employees earned such an award.

Google's website proclaims its unusual modus operandi:

"At lunchtime, almost everyone eats in the office café, sitting at whatever table has an opening and enjoying conversations with Googlers from different teams. Our commitment to innovation depends on everyone being comfortable sharing ideas and opinions. Every employee is a hands-on contributor, and everyone wears several hats. Because we believe that each Googler is an equally important part of our success, no one hesitates to pose questions directly to Larry or Sergey in our weekly all-hands ("TGIF") meetings – or spike a volleyball across the net at a corporate officer."

In keeping with the company's philosophy of casualness, Google's 27,000 employees do not don hierarchical titles, nor do they fit into neat little boxes on tight organizational charts; instead, employees hold generic job titles, such as director or product manager. The culture is so informal that managers can—and often do—show up at meetings in roller-blade gear. Company engineers are encouraged to spend one day each week working on their own ideas and personal projects, which have, over the years, resulted in new products for Google, such as the social networking site Orkut and Google News. Indeed, it's easy to see how Google's "corporate counterculture" is directly responsible for the company rolling out such a wide range of products so regularly.[226]

Environmental Innovation

The counterculture mentality also reveals itself in Google's lesser known although still substantial sustainability footprint, which rests in the hands of Bill Weihl. Weihl heads the firm's corporate social responsibility and green efforts and is leading the company on a path to make renewable energy cheaper than coal through a mix of internal research and external investments. To reach this goal, Google has invested $45 million dollars in solar, thermal, wind, and advanced geothermal energies, plus "enablers" such as green energy transmission and distribution. The company must walk a fine line between investing in renewable energy and staying true to its core business strategy, which is advertising and running the online search engine. During an interview, Bill Weihl discussed Google's philosophy on the matter:

"I've seen many companies make the mistake of deciding they have very constrained resources and they focus everything on their core business, the

---

[226] Sara Goo. "Building a Googley Workforce" Washington Post Oct 26, 2006; Douglas Edwards. I'm Feeling Lucky: The Confessions of Google Employee Number 59. Houghton Mifflin Harcourt. 2011

stuff that's relevant for the next two quarters or the next year. That works for a little while, and if you're in a horrible downturn or a big crunch, you may have no choice, but I think that it's really important to invest for the long term and it's important to invest some percentage for the world, the philanthropy we're doing." [227]

In 2007, the company launched its RechargeIT program to promote electric, plug-in hybrid vehicles, installed solar panels at the Googleplex headquarters, and set a company goal to become completely carbon-neutral. Google also joined with 30 other companies including Lenovo and Microsoft as well as consumers and non profits to create the "Climate Savers Computing Initiative," a move intended to reduce CO2 emissions by improving the power efficiency and reducing energy consumption. In the same year, the company also launched the Google Earth Outreach, which is designed to help nonprofit organizations use Google Earth to advocate their causes.

Google's RE<C [renewable energy cheaper than coal] strategy is also noteworthy, being "an initiative designed to create electricity from renewable sources that are cheaper than coal. The initial focus is on support for solar thermal power and wind power technologies." In addition, the company was among the first to install Bloom Energy's space age bloom boxes.[228]

In 2008, Google released Clean Energy 2030, "a proposal to wean the U.S. off of coal and oil for electricity use and to reduce automobile oil use by 40 percent by 2030." The plan could generate billions in savings as well as millions of green jobs. Google also shows its concern for environmental issues with Ocean, a new feature on Google Earth "that provides a 3D look at the ocean floor and information about one of the world's greatest natural resources."

The company's efforts to support its people and the environment is complemented by Google.org, a charitable arm of Google created to address social challenges and serve the public good by finding "engineering solutions to global challenges such as climate change, clean energy, and global health."

---

[227] http://www.youtube.com/watch?v=kvEBsnudveI

[228] See www.bloomenergy.com/ and www.wired.com/epicenter/2011/01/bloom-box-cost/

Page and Brin had always intended that their 'experiment in active philanthropy' would one day have an even greater impact on the world than it did on Google itself. They structured Google.org so that in addition to traditional grant making, communities could also invest in for- profit companies, advocate for policies and, most important, tap into Google's strengths: its employees, products and technologies." The company today commits resources from Google's profits, equity and substantial employee time to philanthropic efforts, operating with the intention "to use the power of information and technology to address the global challenges of our age."

Among other worthwhile causes, Google.org supports its community and world through:

- The Google Research Awards full-time faculty pursuing research in areas of mutual interest.
- The Google PhD Fellowship Program, recognizing outstanding graduate students and encouraging students, primarily women and minorities, to pursue computer science and technology studies and to become active role models and leaders.
- BOLD Scholarships, which are diversity internships that encourage historically under-represented groups in the technology industry to explore new career opportunities.
- Holiday gifts, such as its $20 million donation in 2010 to charities around the globe that had been stretched thin by increasing requests for help during a time of lower donations.
- Google employee matching, which provides up to a $12,000 company match for each employee's annual charitable contributions.
- Community Affairs, which makes local donations wherever Google has offices and data centers.[229]

Google funds such activities and global infrastructure-type projects around the world, such as Google Flu Trends, Google Earth Engine, and Google Crisis Response.[230]

---

[229] www.google.org.
[230] www.google.org.

Don't Be Evil

In 2001, Paul Buchhart, a Google engineer, coined the now iconic phrase "Don't Be Evil." His remark, made in the context of a forum discussion around the company's values, insinuated that Google should not be a ruthless, take-no-prisoners monopolist like its arch-rival Microsoft; instead, Buchhart meant, Google should behave ethically.

The company summarized its ethical commitments in what it calls "Google Inc.'s 10 Principles." [231]

GOOGLE INC.'S 10 PRINCIPLES

1. *Focus on the user and all else will follow-- the ultimate goal is to serve the customer and to provide the best user experience possible.*
2. *It's best to do one thing really, really well.*
3. *Fast is better than slow- time is money and there is nothing more discouraging than wasting it.*
4. *Democracy on the web works.*
5. *You don't need to be at your desk to need an answer.*
6. *You can make money without doing evil.*
7. *There is always more information out there.*
8. *The need for information crosses all borders*
9. *You can be serious without a suit.*
10. *Great just isn't good enough*

Can Google Remain a Good Company?

Despite this proclamation, Google's "goodness" has been questioned. Was Google evil in digitizing copyrighted books, or in cooperating with censorship in China? The China episode is revealing. Initially, Google pushed back against government censorship by alerting users when search results were blocked due to Chinese government policy. Then, after hackers breached Google's server and gained access to the accounts of human rights

---

[231] www.google.com/ About Google/ Our Philosophy

activists, the company shut down www.Google.china. Google believed that in accord with its principles, providing access by increasing the flow of information benefitted the Chinese people.

Perhaps Steven Levy, Wired magazine's senior writer best summarized the complexity of the issues surrounding Google's goodness when he wrote that "Google professed a sense of moral purity...but it seemed to have a blind spot regarding the consequences of its own technology on privacy and property rights." In fact, Google questions whether existing laws which fail to protect universal access to information truly benefit the public.[232] In its attempts to open the Web, Google has also been subject to anti-trust investigations, seemingly instigated by Microsoft.

As Google grows and its reach spreads even further, the company will be challenged to maintain its high standards and stick to its principles.

In an interview, Google's CEO Eric Schmidt discussed three possible paths for the future of the Internet. The first is that negative issues, like identity theft, could lead to the regulation of online creativity. The second is that firms will emerge to manage negative issues, and those firms, and creativity, will be somewhat regulated. The third is that Internet will be free and open to everyone, and that everyone will be free to share their ideas with the rest of the world. Although the third scenario does not account for the evil that exists in our world, Google still hopes for it, and is creating policies and working with governments to try to bring it to pass.

---

[232] James Gleick. "How Google Dominates Us." New York Review. Aug 18, 2011 p 26

CHAPTER 20

BUILDING THE FUTURE: NEW CORPORATE MODELS

"We need a new business model, don't we? The corporations we've got are told by law that they have to pursue one exclusive objective, which is to maximize profit. And that singular command is not only inconsistent with the broader yearnings of so many people, but it also has proven to be a deeply troubling public policy that creates terrible incentives and results. Think about the BP Oil spill, the collapsing mines of the Massey Company in West Virginia and the multi-trillion dollar nightmare on Wall Street. We need a business model for companies that want to change the way that business thinks and acts in the world."[233]

Maryland State Senator Jamie Raskin

The good news is that in addition to all these great companies we've examined over the course of this book, progress is being made towards the reinvention of the corporate legal entity and reprioritizing the connection between business and the greater good. Legislation in both the United States and the United Kingdom is responding to the need to reform the corporation and make it responsive to social and environmental needs. This movement builds on the base of a movement toward corporate social responsibility which began in the latter part of the 20th century, which emerged largely to protect firms' reputations.[234]

---

[233] Quoted in B Corporation Annual Survey 2009
[234] Michael Porter and Mark Kramer. "Creating Shared Value". Harvard Business Review. Jan-Feb. 2011 p. 65

Attorney Joel Bakan, author of the book The Corporation put it bluntly. "What I know as an attorney is that the corporation is set up by statute so that managers and directors must serve the best interest of the shareholder. The courts have interpreted those interests as creating wealth, bottom line. So it's actually illegal for a manager or director to do anything that subtracts, at least in the long term, from shareholder returns."

Why We Need to Re-invent the Corporation?

But the profit-centric focus of the corporation has not always been the law. Until the late 19th century, corporate law in the United States was intended to protect the public interest, not the interests of corporate shareholders. Forming a corporation required an act of a state legislature. And corporations were required to comply with the purposes expressed in their charters. Yet corporations still looked for shortcuts and for ways

> We need a new corporate model because in the United States and many countries around the world it is against corporate law for companies to put the public interest first. Companies seeking to promote social aims are subject to legal constraints restricting their ability to access financial markets.

to increase their profits. To avoid bureaucracy and compliance issues, many private firms chose alternate corporate forms such as limited partnerships or trusts like Rockefeller's Standard Oil Trust. State governments, led by Delaware and New Jersey, discovered opportunities to increase their tax revenues by enacting more permissive corporate laws that would attract companies to incorporate in their states, ultimately deciding that the corporation's principle allegiance was not to the community but to their shareholders. [235]

---

[235] The critical moment, however, came when the United States Supreme Court granted corporations a plethora of rights they had not previously recognized or enjoyed, deeming charters "inviolable," and labeling the Corporation an "artificial person," possessing both individuality and immortality. The Court then delivered the crowning blow to public interest through an 1866 case in which the justices interpreted the 14th Amendment to the Constitution in such a way so as to result in corporations being regarded as "persons" having the same rights as human beings.

This legal form has been in part the source of a good deal of corporate malfeance such as Enron's scams to increase its stock price and JP Morgan's development of credit default swaps to rid itself of toxic assets. The for-profit entity, as the engine that drives companies to operate efficiently, seems to have run off the rails.

Allen White, a cofounder and former CEO of the United Nation's Global Reporting Initiative, calls for a return to the original concept of a corporation as "an entity authorized by the government to harness private interests—innovation, competitiveness and wealth creation—to serve the public interest."[236] He questions the excessive role of shareholder interests in determining what companies do and how they do it, concluding that "the notion of the company as the property of passive, remote, and transient shareholders is anathema to creating a culture of social responsibility," and that "we should [instead] encourage ownership structures that align with the concept of the public interest."[237] White further believes that to affect the necessary turnaround, we need to revise our corporate laws so that considering non-shareholder interests are a legal responsibility of company directors.

Susan MacCormac, partner with the international legal firm Morrison and Foerster, expressed similar thoughts to the Summit on the Future of the Corporation. In her conference paper, she wrote: "the prevailing corporate form focuses on maximizing profit for the shareholders at the expense of other stakeholders—especially employees, the community in which it operates, and the natural environment. Even corporations that strive to integrate corporate social responsibility (CSR) into operations face constraints on their ability to pursue deep social responsibility, primarily as a result of the fiduciary obligations of their boards of directors."[238]

Peter Blom, chairman of the Executive Board of Triodos Bank sees that we need "a legal framework that would support a stakeholder approach ... we need more innovations in this field." By that he means the interests of all parties who are affected by a corporation's actions—its employees, the

---

[236] Allen White, "Confessions of a CSR Champion," *Stanford Social Innovation Review* 7, no. 1 (2009): 31
[237] White 2009 p. 31
[238] Susan H. Mac Cormac, "The Emergence of New Corporate Forms," in *Paper Series on Corporate Design*, ed. Allen White and Marjorie Kelly (Boston: Corporation 20/20, 2007), 9:88.

communities where it is located, its suppliers, in addition to the shareholders and managers—need to be represented.[239]

B-Corp : A New Corporate Form

Fortunately, new structures that could facilitate a returned connection between corporate action and the public interest are emerging. Entrepreneurial groups such as B Lab and Corporation 20/20 are redefining corporate organizing principles to create a vision more consistent with humanistic and spiritual values. Corporation 20/20, which I mentioned earlier, is a think tank of 170 leaders from business, labor, law, civil society and government, leaders who seek to develop corporate forms that support a paradigm in which corporations help to meet environmental, economic and social imperatives. Its New Principles for Corporate Design, describe what a socially responsible corporation should and should not do.

Perhaps the most promising model is the B Corporation, a new form of business assumed by a growing network of over 500 companies that brand themselves as beneficial to society. (The "B" in B Corporation stands for "beneficial." B-Lab certifies B-Corporations.) Speaking at the founding meeting of B-Lab, the non-profit which certifies B-Corps in San Francisco, which I attended, co-founder Jay Coen Gilbert declared to an audience of leaders from over 100 companies: "We are setting out tonight to transform the economic landscape. We foresee an economic democracy which will harness private interests to serve the public interest, earning fair returns for shareholders, but not at the expense of the legitimate interests of other stakeholders and without compromising the ability of future generations to meet their needs."

Companies designated as B Corporations undergo a rigorous screening across five categories of social and environmental performance standards and are required to incorporate stakeholder, not shareholder, governance provisions into their legal charter. The idea behind B-Corp is to create a corporate charter under existing law working to bring together standards, legal structures and values to create a brand for companies beneficial to

---

[239] "MIT Green Hub and Peter Blom" April 27,2009. www.presencing.com. Retrieved July 5, 2011

society. As of the beginning of 2012, there were about 500 Certified B Corporations with over $2.5 billion in revenues from 60 distinct industries operating in the US.

The foundation of the B Corporation is a comprehensive ratings system based on a detailed survey of company practices with respect to accountability and governance, work environment and employee compensation, consumer benefit, service to the community and environmental issues including energy use and supply chain.[240]   B Corporations are audited every two to three years. But companies can receive help from a series of B Resource Guides created through a research partnership with Columbia Business School's Research Initiative on Social Entrepreneurship (RISE see www.riseproject.org)

B Lab, the organization, which certifies B Corporations, has developed the B Impact Rating System that assesses corporate impact on employees, consumers, community and the environment. The 200-point rating system is based upon a company's response to 213 metrics about its policies, business practices and strategy.

The B Corporation survey includes questions such as:

- *Are financial controls in place to ensure the accuracy of reporting and elimination of fraud?*
- *Does the company actively recycle?*
- *Does the company evaluate their managers in writing on social and environmental goals?*
- *What is the impact of your product on your customers? Does it directly or indirectly preserve the environment?*
- *Has the company explicitly integrated social performance into its written company mission?*
- *Does the company use methods of production or service delivery that preserve the environment (e.g. cradle-to-cradle certified production)?[241]*

---

[240] The survey is managed by a nine-member Standards Advisory Council, which includes only one member of the B-Lab management team.

[241] Balance is important; while the scoring does not require perfection, a B Corporation cannot score very low in any one category. There are many examples of companies that star in one area, say, in giving to the community, but fail in another, such as in protecting the environment. Overall, a company scoring 80 points on a 200-point scale earns the right to use the B Corporation logo.

To become a B Corporation, a company must embed its commitment to social responsibility in its articles of incorporation. Recent waves of consolidation have changed the character and threatened the integrity of smaller socially responsible companies such as Ben and Jerry's and Stoneyfield Farms when they were acquired by large corporations. For example, in 2004 the widely popular Craigslist sold 28.4 percent of the company to Delaware based eBay. Just three years later, eBay filed a lawsuit against Craigslist that would prevent it "from acquiring founder Craig Newmark's shares when he dies and potentially overriding Craigslist's community-minded mission. [In 2010] a Delaware judge ruled in eBay's favor, stating that stockholder wealth maximization is the only endgame for Delaware corporations [which is] not consistent with the directors' fiduciary duties under Delaware law."[242] What this means is that although a company may be founded and operate on the principle of benefitting all stakeholders, any stockholder can invalidate that intention asserting that it violates the rights of stockholders to demand that the company act solely to maximize shareholder wealth regardless of the impact on employees, the environment or the community.

To preserve corporate integrity despite new ownership or management, a B Corporation must write into its governing documents its duty to "take into due consideration the impact of its decisions not only on its shareholders, but also on its employees, suppliers, community and the environment."[243] In doing so, a company states as part of its official policy that its managers must consider the interests of employees, of the community, and of the environment instead of only shareholders stock value.[244]

But this idea of goodness can easily be misleading. Companies use and abuse it in their marketing and advertising all the time. Witness instances of green-washing, when a company makes false claims about the sustainability

[242] 2011 B Corporation Annual Report. Published as a supplement to Sustainable Industries Spring 2011.
[243] Jay Coen Gilbert, October 2, 2009, quoting from the B Corp Legal Framework in his "Due Consideration and the Supreme Court" blog post available at http://blog.bcorporation.net/2009/10/due-consideration-and-the-supreme-court/
[244] Hannah Clark, "A New Kind of Company: B Corporations Worry About Stakeholders, Not Just Shareholders," in *Leading Organizations: Perspectives for a New Era, 2nd Edition,* ed. Gill R. Hickman (Thousand Oaks, CA: SAGE Publications, 2010), 616.

of its products such as BP which spent millions of dollars branding themselves as a green technology leader while taking decisions which led to the biggest and most destructive oil spill in world history or Sara Lee which ran advertisements touting their "Eco Grain," claiming falsely that the eco grain used in their bread is more sustainable than organic grain. It is critical to have real criteria, standards and metrics for measuring and substantiating corporate sustainability and accountability. In today's "green is good" climate, as Deborah Hirsh of B-Lab explains, "Consumers want to know the difference between good business and deceptive marketing"—or, rather, the difference between what is truly good business and what is simply good marketing. In the same way that the Leadership in Energy and Environmental Design (LEED) rating system has become the standard of certification in the building trades, and as the US government's definition of organic foods has broadened the base of organic food sales and comprehension, thereby shifting the base of an entire industry, B Corporation certification is intended to gain traction as a signifier of good business. [245]

B-CORPORATION PRINCIPLES

- The purpose of the corporation is to harness private interests to serve the public interest.
- Corporations shall earn fair returns for shareholders, but not at the expense of the legitimate interests of other stakeholders.
- Corporations shall operate sustainably, meeting the needs of the present generation without compromising the ability of future generations to meet their needs.
- Corporations shall distribute their wealth equitably among those in the value chain who contribute to its creation.
- Corporations shall be governed in a manner that is participatory, transparent, ethical, and accountable.
- Corporations shall not infringe on other universal human rights.

---

[245] However, the concept is not without limitations. The charter of a B Corporation may prohibit activities that other companies readily engage in, leading entrepreneurs to choose less efficient solutions or requiring them to engage in more complex negotiations to execute strategies. These unique requirements could put B Corporations at a competitive disadvantage.

New Legal Changes - Corporation for the 21st Century

Progress is being made towards the redesign of the corporate entity and its accountability. In the United States and the United Kingdom significant reform of corporate law is underway. As of 2011 Maryland, Vermont, New Jersey and California had passed legislation to enable benefit corporations that "pursue a mission that goes beyond making a profit for owners and investors." Importantly, it also provides legal protection for board members that consider social and environmental issues when making decisions on behalf of the corporation. As of this writing, nine other states are considering similar legislation. [246]

The Minnesota Responsible Business Corporation Act would allow a company to add the letters SRC after its corporate name, indicating that it is a Socially Responsible Corporation. The legislation is intended to permit companies to integrate a dual focus on financial success and social responsibility. The SRC would have to consider the interests of the stockholders, customers and creditors, as well as the public interest and the long and short-term interests of stakeholders. It would also no longer be required by law, as corporations are now, to maximize short-term profits. Moreover, employees elect a percent of the members of the board of directors and the company would be required to issue an annual public interest report.[247]

The low-profit limited liability company (L3C) is another entity form that promises a for-profit company with a non-profit soul. A variant of the limited liability company, this corporate form, recognized in all 50 states,

---

[246] Legislation is moving forward with strong bi-partisan support in Virginia, North Carolina, Pennsylvania, New York, Michigan, and Hawaii. Read more: http://charitylawyerblog.com/2010/04/21/maryland-first-state-to-recognize-socially- responsible-benefit-corporation/#ixzz1D9aaDFK1 and May 19, 2010 Vermont Legislation No. 113. Retrieved from www. .leg.state.vt.us/docs/2010/Acts/ACT113.pdf retrieved Feb 6, 2011.

[247] Senator John Marty and Representative Bill Hilty introduced the bill as Senate File 0510 and House File 0398. The bill creates a new section of law for an alternative kind of corporation, the SR (socially responsible) corporation.

    1. Directors will have an affirmative duty to all stakeholders, 2. Employees and representatives of the public interest will be on the Board of Directors, 3. Directors will be protected from shareholder suits when they choose to consider other stakeholders and the public interest, 4. Socially Responsible investors and consumers will know where to invest their money, and 5. Socially Responsible Companies will be protected from hostile takeover. www.c4cr.org retrieved Feb 6, 2011

allows companies to use profits to finance social activities including low-cost housing, urban redevelopment, and educational programs, as well as to pay modest dividends to investors.

All of these corporate forms parallel British reforms enacted in 2005 creating the community interest company (CIC). As Mac Cormac explains, "A CIC is a limited liability company that is designed for use by those who want to conduct a business for the community benefit, and not purely for financial advantage."[248] A CIC must pass a Community Interest Test to ensure that it operates in the public interest and it must file an annual report detailing how it spends its funds. Although a non-profit charity cannot qualify as a CIC, it may invest in or own one.

In 2011 California's State Assembly passed legislation to create a new corporate form. AB 361 (Huffman) created the Benefit Corporation which puts into legal practice the B-Corp values giving entrepreneurs and investors an additional choice when determining which corporate form is most suitable to achieve their objectives.

The law creates the legal framework for firms to remain true to their social goals. To qualify, a firm must have an explicit social or environmental mission, and undertake a legally binding responsibility to take into account the interests of workers, the community and the environment as well as its shareholders, and it must publish independently verified reports on its social and environmental impact alongside its financial results. [249]

The Benefit Corporation is a new class of corporation that has a corporate purpose of creating a material positive impact on society and the environment and not just the welfare of the shareholders. In addition, it redefines fiduciary duty to require the board of directors to consider the interests of employees, community, and the environment. Each year a

---

[248] The law allows boards of directors to consider: *The long-term and the short-term interests of the corporation and its shareholders. The effects that the corporation's actions may have in the short-term or the long-term upon any of the following :A. The prospects for potential growth, development, productivity, and the profitability of the corporation . B. The economy of the state and the nation. C..The corporation's employees, suppliers, customers, and creditors. D .Community and societal considerations. E .The environment.*

[249] The Economist. "B Corps Firms with benefits A new sort of caring, sharing company gathers momentum" Jan 7, 2012

company incorporated as a Benefit Corporation must issue an annual report on its overall social and environmental performance using independent, credible, and transparent third party standards. In view of the size and importance of California's economy in the United States as well as the world, this legislation represents a major achievement toward establishing the legal basis for 21st Century corporations which will certainly lead to the expansion of the number of good companies.

Clearly, the opportunity exists to create new legal forms and solutions through which companies and non-profits can work jointly to meet long-term social and economic needs while promoting and facilitating the growth of a range of beneficial enterprises that serve the common good.

CHAPTER 21

LESSONS FROM GOOD COMPANIES

In the Talmud a rabbi named Ben Zoma asks a powerful question.

"Who is wise?"

The answer: "The one who learns from all people." You should learn from all people, ... you have much to gain from seeking and appreciating the wisdom in every person you encounter.

That's powerful and crucial advice for anyone who wants to run a business. Joining forces with others is what makes it worth doing. That's what makes it meaningful and fulfilling.

NOAH ALPER, FOUNDER OF NOAH'S BAGELS

Now that you have read all of these inspiring stories about good businesses, you might be thinking, I would like to start my own good business. Where do I begin? What are the lessons I can take from these stories? What do they have to tell me? In this concluding chapter, we'll discuss the keys you need to start a good company.

In her book, *The Successful Business Plan*, Rhonda Abrams makes the point that "Every company must make money. You can't stay in business unless you eventually earn a profit. However, studies of business success over time have shown that companies that emphasize goals in addition to making money succeed better and survive longer than companies who's sole motivation is money ... Articulating your company's values to employees, supporters, and even your customers can strengthen their commitment to your business."[250]

Step 1. Start with a Vision

I think of my experience as a co-founder of LIDERE in Brazil, which launched in 1995. LIDERE, which stands for Leadership Development for Schools, equipped schools in Northeastern Brazil to manage a particularly difficult social reality—poor facilities, inadequate knowledge of administrative techniques, and a lack of trained teachers—by providing training in leadership, team-building, and shared governance. LIDERE began with a transformative vision of better schools and better education for children in poor communities. And in fact, in each school we began with a visioning session with the teachers, parents and administrators of what they would like for their school. We invited them to close their eyes and dream their future. To imagine flying over their school as they hope it could be five or ten years into the future. We wrote those visions down to guide our progress.

When Chip Conley began building the Joie de Vivre group of hotels, he too started with a vision of his product. He asked what did consumers need? Was it just a room to stay in, or was it something more? Conley found that consumers wanted more than just a room to stay in, they wanted an experience. He set out to make it fun, yet connected to a greater cause. He would provide guests with an educational experience, increasing their knowledge of sustainability, encouraging them to reach higher goals - something that appealed to a need for meaning and fun, something hotel guests had never before imagined would be available. He did not create a need, but catered to a deep-felt natural need.

Clif Bar began with a vision of a tasty nutritional energy bar for cyclists and mountain climbers. But the company has continuously reinvented its original product to meet the evolving needs of consumers and to appeal to a larger market. "We want to keep our mojo for the long haul and believe we can do that by attending carefully to natural demand, using ingredients that

---

[250] Rhonda Abrams. The Successful Business Plan. 4th Edition. The Planning Shop. 2003. P.9.

help us tread lightly on the earth, and staying intimately connected with our consumers."[251]

A good company generates value for its customers through its product and service offerings. If a company's product or service does not address a genuine need or desire, few people will buy it.

Luiz de Cunha's dream to create natural beauty products in 1969, led him to begin selling cosmetics in a small corner store in Sao Paulo, Brazil where he had daily contact with his customers. He talked to them, listened to them, and began to understand the importance of dialogue in his approach to business and beauty. When in 1970 Cunha met Guilherme Leal and Pedro Pasos the three men formed a partnership and together built their philosophy of relationships that formed the company that became Natura Cosmeticos. They shared a vision of life as a series of relationships in which everything is connected; a network, and a belief that they could produce a variety of cosmetics and fragrances sourced from small villages in the Amazon. The founders then communicated their vision to and provided training for their sales associates through frequent workshops and recognition through recognition programs.

A good company meets its goals by actively serving others - customers, suppliers, employees and the broad community. Like Triodos Bank, it produces a product or service that benefits its consumers and society. Triodos Bank has been exceptionally successful because it only finances activities that create positive social, environmental, or cultural benefits for its depositors. Triodos does not support companies that earn any revenue from items it deems dangerous, such as environmentally hazardous chemicals, pornography, tobacco, and weapons.

Step 2: Define Your Business Model

Values are fine as drivers and motivators, but for a business to survive it must make money in excess of its expenses. It must generate a profit. A company's business model is the method it uses to generate revenues and margins to cover the cost of operations. The company must have adequate

---

[251] Gary Erikson. Raising the Bar. Jossey-Bass.2004.P.257

average monthly cash receipts or cash flow to meet its average expenses. If you have a business that fails to generate a profit, as Mary O'Connor, founder of the Sustainable Leadership Institute tells her clients, then "you don't have a business, you have an expensive hobby!"

Once you have established your vision and identified a product or service that meets the needs of customers, prudent management of expenses is critical. Gary Erickson notes that the company doesn't exist just to make a profit, but it can't survive without it. But he adds sagaciously "if we want to sustain our business. We feel an obligation to our employees and our consumers to make sure ClifBar Inc. is viable and lasting. So we don't push Clif Bar to grow unnaturally, but rather to sustain itself over time." [252]

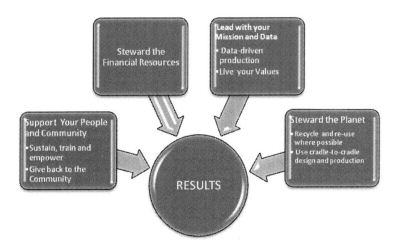

FIGURE 20.1 Components Of A Robust Business Model

Figure 20.1 illustrates how the components of the good company can be put into practice. Prudent management or stewarding the company's financial resources allows the company to earn a sufficient profit margin to pay for expenses and provide a cushion in case things don't work out as expected.

Rather than going for break-neck growth, the company opts to strike a balance by choosing a rate of growth that provides career opportunities for

[252] Raising the Bar p.258.

employees without compromising the values on which the company rests. Stewarding a business requires paying constant attention to profit and loss, cash flow, inventory, and protecting the gross margin.

Non-profits also need Robust Business Models

When Delancey Street founder Mimi Silbert recognized and wanted to fill a need in her community for a program to rehabilitate felons and drug addicts, she knew she would have to find a way to pay for it. She explored new commercial approaches to raising funds, such as forming community partnerships and starting mission-related businesses. To provide revenue to support Delancey Street's programs, Silbert launched a business training school, a moving business and school, and a restaurant that would teach former felons marketable skills, all the while generating revenues to run Delancey Street's social programs.

In 1973, the non-profit was awarded a federal charter with the National Credit Union Administration as the first credit union run by and for ex-convicts. Corporations donated products. Friends donated money. People started using Delancey Street's moving services and buying trees from its Christmas tree lots. The moving firm grew from one small, rented truck to a number of big rigs, and the moving school began to send graduates out into the community to drive trucks. Through its business model, the Delancey Street community was helping turn lives around and bettering itself in the process. Since its founding, Delancey Street has established a dozen successful subsidiaries to help solve social problems while training residents in marketable skills. Together, these successful commercial enterprises provide 60 percent of the organization's annual budget and have proved the success of a hybrid business model that combines profit and non-profit elements, emphasizing both mission and the need for each enterprise to be profitable.

Step 3. Train, Sustain, and Empower your Employees

Leaders of good companies model high standards by being role models and by doing the best for all members of the organization. James Kouzos and

Barry Posner, authors of *The Leadership Challenge,* identify several features of exceptional leaders. They inspire us with a shared vision. They give us space to exchange our spirits; space to give and receive beautiful things such as ideas, openness, dignity, joy, healing, and a sense of inclusion. Exceptional leaders lead by example, inspiring us to learn and to reach our potential. Good leaders recognize and reward performance, encouraging our hearts and good companies enhance our spirit.

The symbol for business in Chinese represents the phrase 'life's meaning.' If you can provide meaning to your employees' lives you will attract quality employees.

Stewarding the business means creating an environment in which employees can thrive. A company's commitment to supporting a balanced lifestyle by creating a good, healthy, and fun place to work can pay substantial dividends.

There are many ways a company can demonstrate that it values employees, including providing adequate pay and benefits, good working conditions, and profit sharing. Still, surveys consistently tell us that listening to employees and involving them in decisions is what motivates employees to do their best. Bill George, CEO of the global medical device maker Medtronic says it this way: "People don't come to work to earn money for themselves and the company. They come to work because the product does something worthwhile, and this is what gets people inspired." [253]

ClifBar strives to provide fair compensation, meaningful work, and superior benefits. The company offers health coverage, an employee stock ownership plan [ESOP], and a three month paid sabbatical every seven years. Now, your company may not be able to do all that on day one, but by stating your aspirations and values, you will attract quality employees.

Each year the North Bay Business Journal surveys companies in the north of the San Francisco Bay Area to identify companies regarded by their employees as the best places to work. Environmental consulting company, Sonoma Technology, Inc. [STI], is a five-time winner in this contest.

---

[253] Quoted in Chip Conley. *Peak: How Great Companies Get their Mojo From Maslow.*Jossey Bass 2007.

According to the Journal "One of STI's key objectives is to improve and increase communication at every level, while also keeping an eye on the bottom line, ensuring quality and broadening the business base." An employee added 'STI is a great place to work because our president, Lyle Chinkin and all of our managers truly care about us. The firm is run in an open and ethical manner where all 68 employees have an opportunity to work on projects that really make a difference in the lives of our clients and the public.'"[254]

At LIDERE we first trained our graduate-student and volunteer staff in skills and concept needed to succeed. As leaders, we provided training in budgeting, curriculum development and communication, all skills needed to improve the functioning of the schools. We also trained our team to do research on applied school administration. We started with a pilot program of six schools and a series of objectives to strengthen school leadership. The pilot allowed us to test and refine our concepts. As our credibility grew, so did our staff and our reach. Program activities expanded over several years through strategic alliances with community organizations. These, in turn, built credibility as we responded to school and community needs guided by the initial vision. Every month we recognized team members for their work and for our mutual successes. Our motto was "*Nos somos todos brilhantes!*" [Working together we are brilliant.] As a result LIDERE was invited - and paid by the municipal government - to work with more than 80 schools serving some 40,000 students. As a non-profit enterprise associated with the Federal University of Bahia, LIDERE did not earn a profit. Instead, our success translated into accomplished students, additional contracts, recognition as one of the Ford Foundation's top ten projects in Latin America, and publication of a widely used textbook, *A Escola Participativa* [255] now in its ninth edition.

Drake Sadler, founder of Traditional Medicinals, draws his inspiration from philosophy. On a visit to the company headquarters, he told me "The universe is pregnant with opportunities. In the mid 1980's we ran out of cash because we were growing too fast." This is a common problem among small start up businesses; lack of capital to finance growth. "We didn't want

[254] North Bay Business Journal.Sept.26,2011 p 38
[255] A Escola Pariticipativa [The Participatory School]; Editora Vozes, 2005

to borrow from outside investors because in the long run they would want to take out more than they put in. So we did a self-assessment. We had hired some new people who thought differently and challenged us to stay current. So we discussed our strategy with our employees and we admitted our mistakes so that we could all learn from them. This process created a community of trust and honesty in which all employees were empowered."

The company was able to boost production without additional borrowing. Then later, building on this base, Sadler began to sell the company to the employees using a share of the profits generated each year to purchase shares for the employees.

Chip Conley of the Joie de Vivre hotel group recommends listing 10 reasons why someone would want to join your company or organization. If you can't come up with ten reasons, he says, you need to get busy and create them.

Step 4. Partner with the Community

A good company gives back to those who contribute to its creation, both the community and the environment. Consumers today want business leaders to look beyond profits. Gary Erikson says "Community service is important to who we are as a company. I believe it also contributes to sustain our people." Thao Pham, ClifBar's director of human resources put it this way, "I believe that giving back to our community is a privilege, and I will always value the experiences of helping others. Through our 2080 Program [through which employees take on two days of community service at company expense], we have been touched by the warm smiles, the hearty laughs, and the tears of joy and sadness of those we have helped—whether it is a small child facing diabetes or a senior citizen enjoying a warm meal. They have all inspired us to be more courageous and have taught us to be humble."[256]

Give Something Back encourages its employees to partner with the community and participate in social projects and volunteer. GSB employees might sit on nonprofit boards or mentor disadvantaged youth. Alma

---

[256] Gary Erikson. Raising the Bar. Jossey-Bass.2004.P.288

Azarcon, director of Human Resources, has been with GSB for 10 years. She speaks with excitement when she tells you about a particular social activity called "Rebuilding Together" that takes place in Oakland and the larger Bay Area. Through this program, volunteers upgrade homes for the low-income elderly and community centers. The company shares a portion of its profits with nonprofit organizations. The rest is used to support GSB's growth.

"The socially beneficial aspect of our business is certainly a competitive advantage with some customers," said company president Mike Hannigan. "But if you're the procurement officer for a major corporation and you have to explain to your controller the decision to go with an independent supplier called Give Something Back over, say, a Staples or an OfficeMax, that can be a bit of a risk. A lot of prospective customers ask how a company that donates its profits can operate successfully. As survey after survey has shown, most customers would prefer to do business with a vendor that has a positive impact in the community if that opportunity comes at no compromise to them. Once we get past that threshold of proving ourselves it's pretty hard to get us out."

Swiss company Glasi Hergiswil is located on the edge of Lake Lucerne in the Swiss Alps. Founded in 1817 by three brothers, for many years, the factory produced an array of glassware including apothecary bottles, drinking glasses, decanters, food storage containers, and beakers for chemists. A high point in the firm's history occurred when a hostile German Reich surrounded Switzerland during World War II; the factory went into 24-hour-operation mode, producing jars for preserving foods and enabling the Swiss people to survive the long winters. Following the war, with competition from new technologies, glassware became a cheap commodity. Revenues fell and the factory was shuttered. The company had to change. It had to find a new business model.

Partnering with the community of Hergiswil, the company reinvented itself from a manufacturer of low-end glassware to a designer of high-value premium glass art and gifts. Providing employment for more than 100 artisans, the company rose from the ashes and shifted its business model to become one of Europe's leading labels of quality craftsmanship.

Step 5. Be a Steward for the Planet

Osmosis, a day spa in beautiful Sonoma County, California, grew out of Michael Stusser's vision to create a tranquil Japanese bath and spa. In 1989, he found a piece of swampland that had been the site of a dump. He turned the land into a garden. Osmosis attracted clients from around the world, by paying attention to people, the planet, and the community. He invited a team of students from the Presidio School of Management in San Francisco to conduct a sustainability assessment, engaging his staff to identify sustainability-related changes. As a result, Osmosis installed solar collectors and on-demand water heaters to cut electricity usage, built a small pond rich with impurity-extracting plants and filters to save water, and installed a dishwasher to reduce waste from the use of paper products. After these sessions, morale soared, as did customer satisfaction and company profits. Stusser's experiences also led him to found the Green Spa Network, a non-profit trade association devoted to helping the entire spa industry become more sustainable.

Eric Fenster had a multi-faceted vision to start a top quality sustainable restaurant at the heart of a dynamic community center as well as an innovative wilderness program taking adults and children to explore the natural world. With this ambitious project in mind, Fenster returned from five-day desert journey and shared his vision with his old friend Ari Derfel who was managing an outdoor adventure program in San Francisco at the time. Fenster and Derfel's first company, Back to Earth Outdoors organized wilderness leadership programs for inner-city students, yoga backpacking retreats, backpacking cancer fundraisers, and teambuilding experiences. The success of their catered trips led them to open Back to Earth Organic Catering in 2003.

The two founders continued working on the restaurant concept, carefully collecting ideas, materials, and food vendors. From the start, they focused on local, sustainable farmers and artisan food purveyors within a 300 mile range. When the David Brower Center published a request for proposals for a restaurant in its soon-to-open LEED Platinum building in downtown Berkeley, the pair submitted a 65-page proposal. Their bid was accepted.

In 2009 Gather Restaurant opened its doors. The decor highlights re-used materials. For example, the lighting fixtures are shaved and frosted wine bottles, the seat cushions are fashioned from used leather belts, the counters are composed of compressed paper-stone. All produce, meat and seafood are sourced locally using the Monterey Bay Aquarium's sustainable seafood list. In just two years, it's become a top dining spot in the Bay Area. In 2010, the restaurant was named a Top New Restaurant and *Esquire* Magazine selected Executive Chef Sean Baker as Chef of the Year. Gather has become an immediate success and reached baseline profitability after 6 months of operation. They are paving the way toward a successful, sustainable food future.

Step 6. Lead with your Mission and Data

Marc Lesser author of *ZBA: The Zen of Business Administration*, says a good company runs like a gourmet kitchen. It is driven by the thoughtful analysis of carefully collected, timely, and accurate information and exhibits clarity of activity where each cook knows what is being prepared, what is needed and when each ingredient is required. In a kitchen, all the implements are neatly organized. In a good company, the roles are clearly defined and everyone works together in a group effort. In a kitchen, feedback comes from the guests at each meal so that the kitchen staff can address what worked and what didn't work and make adjustments in the menu and preparation of future meals. A business must stay close to its customers and make adjustments to meet their evolving needs.

Companies are valuing systems. They don't just provide us with the goods and services we need; they provide their employees a sense of purpose and connection with colleagues and co-workers. We want companies and leaders who inspire us.

Peter Blom, Chairman of Triodos Bank, is driven by his desire to build a bank that others recognize not only as a good bank that supports good causes like wind and solar energy or organic farming, but also a bank that provides a model that other banks can use and learn from.[257]

---

[257] Address to the Presencing Institute. "MIT Green Hub and Peter Blom" April 27,2009. www.presencing.com

At Traditional Medicinals production systems are data-driven. The company keeps abreast of evolving consumer needs and demands for its natural pharmaceuticals: products must reach and maintain a minimum level of demand and sales. If too few products are sold in a given year, the product may be discontinued. Traditional Medicinals reduces production costs while remaining true to its environmental values, acting on those values through its purchasing and packaging strategies, as well as the installation of solar panels to generate 80 percent of its energy. Together these factors contribute to maintaining or improving profit margins. Continuous improvement is part of the company's strategy.

Putting It Together

Noah's Bagels founder Noah Alper might say that a good company is one that operates honorably. Alper coined the term *business mensch* to characterize a business that operates with integrity, or that acts like a good, decent person. According to Alper, becoming a business mensch - or an honorable business - is an intentional effort that "starts with personal integrity, then it moves to the way you treat your coworkers and employees, and finally it emanates externally, to your relationships with customers, suppliers, competitors and the community."[258]

As discussed in the previous chapter, new structures like California's Benefit Corporations and organizations like B-net that facilitate the spread of good companies which promote the public interest are emerging around the world. These companies—good companies—whose respect for fellow beings and along with careful attention to the financial bottom line provide us with a working model for replacing the unequal power and privilege which have undermined the global economy with an approach based on the concept of partnership.

Take the examples of these companies to heart. Talk about them with your friends, your colleagues and your staff. Diligently apply the lessons within your own firm. And perhaps one day your firm, too, will be recognized and admired as a good company.

---

[258] Noah Alper. Busines Mench. 2011

INDEX

Companies

Subjects

Ford Foundation, 2, 4, 183
Federal University of Bahia, 4, 183
The Looting of America, 9
Low profit limited liability company (L3C), 174
Minnesota Responsible Business Corporation Act, 174
Non-profit, 5, 29, 83, 115-116, 170, 174-175, 181, 183, 191
North Bay Business Journal, 183
Occupy Wall Street, 12, 14
Quadruple bottom line, 24, 96
Robust business model, 180-181
Sonoma State University, 3-4, 42-45, 85, 87, 90-91
Successful Business Plan, 177
Sustainability, 4, 12, 36, 45, 86-87, 90, 92, 118-120, 123-124
Switzerland, 26, 53, 146, 157, 185
United Nations Global Compact, 16, 38
Vision, 178
World health, 47-56, 71-73, 102-106,

People

Abrams, Rhonda, 177-178
Alper, Noah, 177, 188
Anderson, Ray, 30, 117-119, 122-124
Auletta, Ken, 155-159
Balkan, Joel, 168
Bassi,Laurie, 37
Batstone, David, 14
Blom, Peter, 13, 65-66, 169-170, 187-188
Brin, Sergey, 156-158, 162, 164
Brown, Lester, 30
Carlucci, Alessandro, 136, 140
Chinkin, Lyle, 183
Coen-Gilbert, Jay, 17, 170, 172
Conley, Chip, 178, 182, 184
Cohen, Ben, 16, 33
Da Cunha, Luiz, 135-136, 179

Books and Periodicals

APPENDIX

HOW TO PLAN YOUR GOOD COMPANY

Imagine that you are envisioning an enterprise to address an important social, environmental or global need or alternatively, a project that you personally would like to develop.

1. What is the issue or need you would like to address? (State it clearly and concisely)

2. Who are the intended beneficiaries or customers?

3. What is your vision for this project? Imagine that your project were to be wildly successful--describe the outcome.

4. What are three specific objectives you hope to accomplish?

5. What is your business model? How will you generate income to pay for your start-up and monthly expenses?

   a.) Is any other company, non-profit or agency doing something similar? Who are your models and your competitors?

6. What is your marketing plan? How do you plan to identify and reach your clients or customers?

a.) What are your ideas/plans for distributing and advertising your product/service?

b.) What can you do to ensure that your product or service sustains the planet?

7. About how much money would you need in order to get started?

   a.) How might you finance the project?

   b.) What are some possible sources of funds for your project?

8. How will you staff your company? What are three reasons employees would want to work with you?

9. What will you do to ensure that the enterprise serves the community and protects or restores the environment?

10. What are some initial tasks you will need to undertake to begin your project or to get it off and running?

11. Who are some potential allies or partners who could help you with your project?

FOR FURTHER READING

Rhonda Abrams. The Successful Business Plan. 4th Ed. The Planning Shop. 2003

Marc Allen. Visionary Business. New World Library. 1997.

Noah Alper. Business Mensch. Wolfeboro Press. 2009

Christine Arena. Cause for Success. New World Library. 2004

Ken Auletta. Googled. Penguin. 2009.

Laurie Bassie et. al. Good Company: Business Success in the Worthiness Era. Berrett-Koehler. 2011

David Bornstein. How to Change the World: Social Entrepreneurs and the Power of New Ideas. Oxford University Press. 2004

Lester Brown. Plan B 2.0. Norton. 2006

Bo Burlinggame. Small Giants. Penguin. 2005

Deepak Chopra; Seven Spiritual Laws of Success, New World Library. 1993

Ben Cohen and Mal Warwick. Values-driven Business. Berrett-Koehler. 2006

Chip Connely. Peak: How Great Companies Get their Mojo from Maslow. Jossey-Bass. 2007

Mathew and Terces Engelhart. Sacred Commerce. North Atlantic Books. 2008

Marc J. Epstein. Making Sustainability Work. Berrett-Koehler. 2008

Gary Erickson. Raising the Bar. Jossey-Bass. 2004

Daniel Esty and Andrew Winston. Green to Gold. Wiley. 2009

Gil Friend. The Truth about Green Business. FT Press. 2009

Joan Gallos. Business Leadership. Jossey Bass. 2008

Paul Hawken. Blessed Unrest. Viking. 2007

Paul Hawken. The Ecology of Commerce. HarperBusiness. 1993

Darcy Hitchcock and Marsha Willard. The Business Guide to Sustainability. Earthscan. 2007

Jeffrey Hollender. What Matters Most. Basic Books. 2004

Tony Hseih. Delivering Happiness. Business Plus Publishers. 2010

James Kouzos and Barry Posner. The Leadership Challenge. Jossey Bass. 1995.

Les Leopold. The Looting of America: How Wall Street's Game of Fantasy Finance Destroyed our Jobs, Pensions, and Prosperity. Chelsea Green. 2009

Marc Lesser. ZBA-The Zen of Business Administration. New World Library.2005

Steven Levy. In the Plex: How Google Thinks, Works and Shapes our Lives. Simon and Schuster. 2011

Hunter Lovins and Boyd Cohen. Climate Capitalism. Hill and Wang.2011

Kevin Lynch and Julius Walls. Mission, Inc. The Practitioner's Guide to Social Enterprise. Berrett-Koehler. 2009

Arnaud Maitland. Master Work. Dharma Publishers. 2000

Joel Makower. Strategies for the Green Economy. McGraw-Hill. 2009

Kelly McElhaney. Just Good Business. Berrett-Koehler. 2008

Pavithra Mehta and Suchitra Shenoy. Infinite Vision: How Aravind Became the World's Greatest Business Case for Compassion. Berrett-Koehler, 2011

Brian Nattrass and Mary Altomare. Dancing with the Tiger. New Society Publishers. 2002.

Jacob Needleman. Why Can't We Be Good. Penguin. 2007

CK Prahalad. The Fortune at the Bottom of the Pyramid. Wharton School Publishing. 2005

Geshe Michael Roach. The Diamond Cutter: The Buddha on Strategies for Managing Your Business and Your Life. Doubleday. 2000

Ricardo Semler. Maverick. Warner Books. 1995

Randall Stross. Planet Google. Free Press .2008

Tom Szaky. Revolution in a Bottle: How Terra-cycle is Redefining Green Business. Penguin. 2009

Woody Tasch. Inquiries into the Nature of Slow Money. Chelsea Green Press. 2008

Siva Vaidhyanathan. The Googleization of Everything. University of California Press. 2011

Sarah Van Gelder. This Changes Everything: Occupy Wall Street. Berrett-Koehler. 2011

Wilford Welch. Tactics of Hope: how Social Entrepreneurs are Changing our World. Earth Aware. 2004

Worldwatch Institute, Erik Assadourian State of the World 2010. Worldwatch Institute. 2010

William Young and Richard Welford. Ethical Shopper. Fusion Press. 2002

ACKNOWLEDGMENTS

So many people helped me in the writing of this book. My colleagues who participated in the Sustainable Enterprise Conference, a broad based community group of business people and community leaders who promote sustainable business in Northern California have been important supporters and sources of inspiration-- especially Oren Wool, Tanya Narath, Terry and Genevieve Taylor, Joey Shepp, and Mary O'Connor. My students in the MBA and EMBA classes on Sustainable Business Strategies provided valuable research assistance. I owe a debt to the many business and thought leaders and CEOs who have given of their time and shared with me their insights—Terry Mollner, Rob Colman, Mike Hannigan, Matt Reynolds, Scott Leonard, Brad Baker, Blair Kellison, John Webbley, Tom Scott, Tom Duryea, Bobbi Beehler, Wes Selke, Michael Stusser, Jeff Edelheit, Rob Turner, Gil Friend, Don Shaffer, Jeff Mendelsohn and Mohit Mukerjee to name just a few. Eric Leenson, Richard Landry and Tina Sciabica of the Social Venture Network opened doors to more information. My colleagues at Sonoma State University Bill Silver, Armand Gilinsky, Merith Weisman, Miriam Hutchins, Kris Wright and Liz Thach provided support and encouragement. In addition, I acknowledge the work of Christina Webber of *Sustainable Industries*, Sharon Shinn of *BizEd*, Eric Nee of the *Stanford Social Innovation Review* and Brad Bollinger of the *North Bay Business Journal* who do so much through their publications to promote our understanding of how business is changing. Jay Coen Gilbert, Bart Houlihan, Andrew Kassoy and Deb Hirsch of B-Net were extremely helpful in sharing information about their work. In Brazil Thomas Simon, Nelson Cerquiera, Ana de Melo Custodio and Celso Greco helpfully provided information about Brazil's efforts to promote good companies. And my colleagues Katia Siqueira de Freitas and Bob Verhine and our many volunteers and staff in the LIDERE program helped me to understand the practice of making the office a place of fun and excitement. Tom and Louisa DiGrazia provided encouragement and support over many years. All of these have been some of the important allies in helping me to develop and ground my insights.

In addition, I owe an especial thanks to my wife Sherry Keith, to Renae Gregoire of The Happy Editor, Kate Farnady, Amanda Schwartz, Andrea Cohen, Suzanne Girot, Heidi Eisips, Terry Mandel, Jocelyn King, Jaren Krchnavi, Joe Rief and Chopin who provided thoughtful comments on some of the many drafts.

Naturally, any errors or oversights are all my own.

ABOUT THE AUTHOR

Robert Girling is a professor in the School of Business and Economics at Sonoma State University. After earning his Ph.D. at Stanford University he worked as an economist with the Government of Jamaica, then later taught at the Federal University of Bahia and the Federal University of Minas Gerais in Brazil, as well as at the University of the West Indies. He has consulted with the World Bank, the United Nations, and the International Center for Research on Women. He is a social entrepreneur who co-founded LIDERE, a school improvement program in Brazil which worked with 80 schools in Northeastern Brazil and a co-founder of the Sustainable Enterprise Conference series which works to promote a 21st Century Sustainable Economy in Northern California. The author of over 50 articles and books including Multinational Institutions and the Third World (1985); Education: Management and Participation (1990); A Escola Participativa (9th ed.) (2006), he has received awards for his teaching and research and served as a Fulbright Senior Scholar

Made in the USA
Charleston, SC
01 December 2016